CliffsNotes™

Machiavelli's
The Prince

By Stacy Magedanz, MLS

IN THIS BOOK

- Learn about the Life and Background of the Author
- Preview an Introduction to the Work
- Explore themes in the Critical Commentaries
- Examine in-depth Character Analyses
- Acquire an understanding of the work with Critical Essays
- Reinforce what you learn with CliffsNotes Review
- Find additional information to further your study in CliffsNotes Resource Center and online at www.cliffsnotes.com

D0011101

IDG Books Worldwide, Inc.
An International Data Group Company
Foster City, CA • Chicago, IL • Indianapolis, IN • New York, NY

About the Author

Stacy Magedanz is a reference librarian in the Pfau Library at California State University–San Bernardino.

Publisher's Acknowledgments

Editorial

Project Editor: Tere Drenth

Acquisitions Editor: Greg Tubach

Glossary Editors: The editors and staff at Webster's New World™ Dictionaries

Editorial Administrator: Michelle Hacker

Production

Indexer: York Production Services, Inc.

Proofreader: York Production Services, Inc.

IDG Books Indianapolis Production Department

CliffsNotes™ Machiavelli's *The Prince*
Published by
IDG Books Worldwide, Inc.
An International Data Group Company
919 E. Hillsdale Blvd.
Suite 300
Foster City, CA 94404
www.idgbooks.com (IDG Books Worldwide Web site)
www.cliffsnotes.com (CliffsNotes Web site)

Library of Congress Control Number: 00-107692

ISBN: 0-7645-8663-7

Printed in the United States of America

10 9 8 7 6 5 4 3 2 1

1O/RV/RR/QQ/IN

Distributed in the United States by IDG Books Worldwide, Inc.

Distributed by CDG Books Canada Inc. for Canada; by Transworld Publishers Limited in the United Kingdom; by IDG Norge Books for Norway; by IDG Sweden Books for Sweden; by IDG Books Australia Publishing Corporation Pty. Ltd. for Australia and New Zealand; by TransQuest Publishers Pte Ltd. for Singapore, Malaysia, Thailand, Indonesia, and Hong Kong; by Gotop Information Inc. for Taiwan; by ICG Muse, Inc. for Japan; by Intersoft for South Africa; by Eyrolles for France; by International Thomson Publishing for Germany, Austria and Switzerland; by Distribuidora Cuspide for Argentina; by LR International for Brazil; by Galileo Libros for Chile; by Ediciones ZETA S.C.R. Ltda. for Peru; by WS Computer Publishing Corporation, Inc., for the Philippines; by Contemporanea de Ediciones for Venezuela; by Express Computer Distributors for the Caribbean and West Indies; by Micronesia Media Distributor, Inc. for Micronesia; by Chips Computadoras S.A. de C.V. for Mexico; by Editorial Norma de Panama S.A. for Panama; by American Bookshops for Finland.

For general information on IDG Books Worldwide's books in the U.S., please call our Consumer Customer Service department at 800-762-2974. For reseller information, including discounts and premium sales, please call our Reseller Customer Service department at 800-434-3422.

For information on where to purchase IDG Books Worldwide's books outside the U.S., please contact our International Sales department at 317-572-3993 or fax 317-572-4002.

For consumer information on foreign language translations, please contact our Customer Service department at 1-800-434-3422, fax 317-572-4002, or e-mail rights@idgbooks.com.

For information on licensing foreign or domestic rights, please phone +1-650-653-7098.

For sales inquiries and special prices for bulk quantities, please contact our Order Services department at 800-434-3422 or write to the address above.

For information on using IDG Books Worldwide's books in the classroom or for ordering examination copies, please contact our Educational Sales department at 800-434-2086 or fax 317-572-4005.

For press review copies, author interviews, or other publicity information, please contact our Public Relations department at 650-653-7000 or fax 650-653-7500.

For authorization to photocopy items for corporate, personal, or educational use, please contact Copyright Clearance Center, 222 Rosewood Drive, Danvers, MA 01923, or fax 978-750-4470.

is a registered trademark under exclusive license to IDG Books Worldwide, Inc. from International Data Group, Inc.

Table of Contents

How to Use This Book

CliffsNotes Machiavelli's *The Prince* supplements the original work, giving you background information about the author, an introduction to the novel, a graphical character map, critical commentaries, expanded glossaries, and a comprehensive index. CliffsNotes Review tests your comprehension of the original text and reinforces learning with questions and answers, practice projects, and more. For further information on Niccolò Machiavelli and *The Prince*, check out the CliffsNotes Resource Center.

CliffsNotes provides the following icons to highlight essential elements of particular interest:

Reveals the underlying themes in the work.

Helps you to more easily relate to or discover the depth of a character.

Uncovers elements such as setting, atmosphere, mystery, passion, violence, irony, symbolism, tragedy, foreshadowing, and satire.

Enables you to appreciate the nuances of words and phrases.

Don't Miss Our Web Site

Discover classic literature as well as modern-day treasures by visiting the CliffsNotes Web site at www.cliffsnotes.com. You can obtain a quick download of a CliffsNotes title, purchase a title in print form, browse our catalog, or view online samples.

You'll also find interactive tools that are fun and informative, links to interesting Web sites, tips, articles, and additional resources to help you, not only for literature, but for test prep, finance, careers, computers, and Internet too. See you at www.cliffsnotes.com!

LIFE AND BACKGROUND OF THE AUTHOR

Personal Background

Niccolò Machiavelli was born in the city of Florence, Italy, on May 3, 1469. His father, Bernardo Machiavelli, was a lawyer, although not a very prosperous one, with much of his income derived from family property rather than his law practice. However, he retained his membership in the lawyers' guild, which was influential in Florentine politics. As a lawyer and a man with a love of literature and writing, Bernardo probably had contacts among the powerful in Florence's political circles, which later provided Niccolò with the opportunity to enter public service. Niccolò would grow up to share his father's literary ambitions.

Very little is know about Machiavelli's early life, but it appears that he received a typical education for a boy of the middle class, learning Latin and reading the classical Roman and Greek authors, particularly the histories. Although Florence was supposed to be a republic, ruled by its leading citizens rather than by lords or princes, during Machiavelli's youth, Florence was effectively controlled by the powerful Medici family, with Lorenzo de Medici, called "the Magnificent," at its head. The Florence of Machiavelli's time was a rich, vibrant city—a center of the arts—of which Lorenzo was a great patron, and a hub of intellectual activity. Florence had an excellent university, where Machiavelli may have listened to lectures, and it is possible he had some contact with Lorenzo's son, Giuliano. Lorenzo's truly magnificent public displays and artistic ventures drained the Medici fortune, and his successor, Piero, proved unpopular. The Medici fell from power in 1494, replaced by Girolamo Savonarola, a Dominican friar who led a charismatic religious government.

No official records of Machiavelli's life appear until 1498, immediately after the fall of Savonarola's government, when he would have been 29. The Florentine republic had been reinstated, and Machiavelli was appointed as secretary of the Second Chancery, a position in which he coordinated relations with Florence's territorial possessions. How he acquired this position is not clear. Participation in the government was expected of all of Florence's leading citizens, but Machiavelli's intelligence and energy must have attracted particular attention among Florence's politicians. Within a month, he also became secretary to the Council of Ten of War, Florence's foreign policy body, in which he functioned as an envoy, traveling extensively around Italy and Europe to negotiate with potential allies, gather information, and do whatever the Ten needed done. Though not officially an ambassador, a position reserved for members of aristocratic families, he was nonetheless a professional diplomat. In 1501, he married Marietta Corsini, with whom he had seven children. Little is known about their relationship beyond the few domestic details that appear in Machiavelli's many letters. Machiavelli appears to have kept more than one mistress during his extensive travels, a practice that would not have been unusual in his time.

Machiavelli would spend 14 years as the "Florentine secretary." During this period, he had opportunities to meet and observe many of the major political figures of the period. Observing and negotiating for the Florentine republic, he visited the courts of Caterina Sforza (in 1499), King Louis XII of France (in 1500, 1504, 1510, and 1511), Cesare Borgia (in 1502 and 1503), Pandolfo Petrucci (in 1503 and 1504), Pope Julius II (in 1503 and 1506), and Emperor Maximilian II (from 1507 to 1508). These visits and his experience in foreign policy would later form the basis of many of the principles he expresses in *The Prince*, and the great personages that he met form the examples from which he draws his lessons. He also became a friend of Piero Soderini, who in 1502 was named *gonfaloniere* (head of the Florentine government) for life. Dismayed by the performance of mercenaries hired by the Florentine government, he persuaded Soderini to back a plan to create a native Florentine militia, very much against the wishes of the Florentine aristocracy. Machiavelli personally supervised the project, overseeing everything from the selection of uniforms to training and maneuvers. He was vindicated in 1509 when the Florentine militia were finally able to take the neighboring city of Pisa after conflicts that had dragged on for 15 years. This marked the high point of Machiavelli's career. However, Florence was a staunch ally of the French, and Pope Julius II was working to drive the French out of Italy. This put Florence into conflict with the pope and his Spanish allies, who sent armies to Florence to remove the Soderini government. Soderini was a man of responsibility and integrity, but Machiavelli would later have harsh words for Soderini's complete inability to control his opponents in Florence or to cut his losses with the French. In 1512, Machiavelli's Florentine militia was cut down by more experienced Spanish troops at the nearby town of Prato, and Soderini was forced to resign in the aftermath. The Medici family returned to Florence, and the people soon demanded that they be put back in power. Soderini was exiled. As a supporter of the Soderini government, Machiavelli was removed from his office by the new regime, fined, and forbidden to travel outside Florentine territory.

A few months later, two young malcontents were arrested and found with a list of supposed conspirators against the Medici. Machiavelli's name was on the list. Although there is no indication he was actually involved, Machiavelli was imprisoned and tortured to extract information. From prison, he wrote two sonnets to Giuliano de Medici, asking him to intercede. He was sentenced to remain in prison pending payment of a fine. However, when Giuliano's uncle, Giovanni, was elected Pope Leo X in March 1513, a general amnesty was declared in celebration, and Machiavelli was released. He retired to the relative safety of his home in the country outside Florence to rest and consider his future. During this time, he wrote many letters to his friend and fellow Florentine diplomat Francesco Vettori, who had been appointed ambassador to Rome, looking for news of the outside world and hoping Vettori could recommend him to the Medici family. In this self-imposed exile, he wrote *The Prince* (*Il Principe*), which distilled his observations about human behavior, leadership, and foreign policy. He dedicated the work to the Medici family in an effort to demonstrate his support, but without success. It was clear by 1515 that the Medici would have nothing to do with him and that his diplomatic career was over.

Over the next ten years, deprived of the political activities that were his life's work, Machiavelli turned his attention to writing. During this period, he produced a treatise on the art of war, one that draws on his experience as organizer of the militia, and a commentary on the writings of the classical Roman historian Livy. Examining Livy's account of the Roman republic, Machiavelli discussed at length the concept of republican government. In contrast with *The Prince*, which supports monarchy or even tyranny, the *Discourses on Livy* are often cited as evidence of Machiavelli's republican sympathies. He also wrote many poems and three comedic plays.

His writing attracted the attention of Cardinal Giulio de Medici, who had for several years been in control of Florence and who commissioned him to write a history of Florence. He worked on his *Florentine History* from 1520 to 1524. Giulio was elected Pope Clement VII in 1523, and Machiavelli presented the finished *History* to him in 1525. Reconciliation with the Medici brought about Machiavelli's brief return to public service. He was put in charge of military arrangements for Clement in Florence. However, Clement foolishly fell for a ploy by his Roman enemies that resulted in his humiliation and the sacking of the papal palace and church of St. Peter. Soon after, Rome fell, and the great Catholic city was terrorized and looted by mostly German Protestant armies. This debacle, and the threat posed to Florence by the advancing forces of Clement's enemies, led the Florentines to depose the Medici family in 1527. Machiavelli, a staunch supporter and lifelong defender of the Florentine republic, was on the losing side once again, now suspected by the republicans for having been in league with the Medici. However, he did not have long to dwell on the irony of his position. He died after an illness in June 1527.

Machiavelli's most famous work was not formally published during his lifetime, although it probably circulated in manuscript copies. *The Prince* was first published in 1532, with the permission of Clement VII. As evidence of its popularity, it went through seven Italian editions in the next twenty years. In 1559, all of Machiavelli's works were put on the "Index of Prohibited Books," a list of books banned by the Catholic church for heresy or immorality. This did nothing to dampen his popularity, and *The Prince* was soon translated into all the major European languages. Today, Machiavelli continues to be recognized as one of the first modern political thinkers and as a shrewd commentator on the psychology of leadership.

Major Works

Decennali, a long poem in two parts on the contemporary history of Florence. First *Decennale*, 1504; Second *Decennale*, 1509 or 1514.

The Prince (*Il principe*), treatise on leadership and political power, 1513.

The Mandrake Root (*Mandragola*), comic play, circa 1516. *Mandrogola* tells the story of young and beautiful Lucrezia, who is married to old and foolish Nicia. Callimaco falls in love with Lucrezia and manages to trick Nicia into giving his full approval for their love affair. It is considered one of the best Italian comedies of this period.

Discourses on Livy (*Discorsi sopra la prima deca ldi Tito Livio*), analysis of the Roman republic, 1514 to 1518.

Andria, comic play, circa 1517. Translation of an original by the Roman playwright Terence.

Art of War (*Dell'Arte della guerra*), treatise on military strategy, 1519 to 1520.

Life of Castruccio Castracani (*Vita di Castruccio Castracani*), biography of a military leader who became ruler of Lucca, 1520.

Florentine History (*Istorie fiorentine*), 1520 to 1524.

Clizia, comic play circa 1525. In *Clizia,* young Cleandro and his aging father, Nicomaco, compete for the love of beautiful Clizia, who is Nicomaco's ward. Considered of lesser quality than *Mandrogola.* Based on *Casina* by the Roman playwright Plautus.

Belfagor, prose novella, date uncertain. Belfagor is a demon who comes to earth to take a wife in order to decide if wives cause men more suffering than Hell.

INTRODUCTION TO THE WORK

Introduction

The Prince is set against the backdrop of the Italian Renaissance, a period of intense activity in art, science, and literature. Rich, sophisticated, and cultured, Italy was the center of intellectual achievement in the Western world, and scholars and artists from all over Europe flocked to it to absorb its heady atmosphere. Even today, the achievements of Italian artists and thinkers are prized for their beauty and originality. Michelangelo and Leonardo da Vinci were Machiavelli's contemporaries, and Florence itself, with its famous cathedral, was one of the capitals of Renaissance art.

It was also a period of religious change. The decadence and corruption of the Catholic church, exemplified by the conduct of Pope Alexander VI, brought about a backlash against Catholic authority. In Germany (at that time, the Holy Roman Empire), the Protestant Reformation was gathering strength, led by Martin Luther, the famous German reformer. In politics, as well, change was brewing. The scattered feudal territories of the medieval period were slowly being brought under centralized leadership, so that the outlines of what would become the modern European nations were becoming visible. The modern concept of the state was being born. War was the ruler's most valuable tool in this struggle to create unified nations. The complexities of European politics during this period can—and indeed have—filled large books.

However, because Machiavelli draws so many of his examples in *The Prince* from contemporary Italian politics, a brief introduction to the tangled history of foreign involvement in Italy is helpful in gaining an understanding of the book. Italy's increasing humiliation in the face of repeated invasions and duplicity from within was a cause of intense resentment to many Italian thinkers. It is this situation that leads Machiavelli to make his impassioned plea for a strong leader to free Italy from "barbarian" domination in Chapter 26.

Italy was composed of five main political powers: Florence, Milan, Venice, the Papal States (including Rome), and the Kingdom of Naples, far in the southern tip of the Italian peninsula. Naples, in particular, had a vexed history, with powers such as France, Spain, and the popes all laying claim to it on various dynastic pretexts. The period prior to 1494 was relatively peaceful and prosperous, with the various Italian powers generally well balanced against each other.

The events that brought such turmoil to Machiavelli's time were set in motion when Ludovico Sforza, Duke of Milan, invited French forces into Italy, offering to support French claims to the Kingdom of Naples, and hoping, in return, to conquer territory from the Venetians with the help of French troops. The French king, Charles VIII, invaded in 1494. Though he was driven out less than a year later by an Italian coalition that Sforza himself joined, on his first entry into Italy, Charles met with practically no resistance, a fact that was not lost on other European leaders. Machiavelli makes note of this in Chapter 12, when he mentions that Charles was able to conquer Italy with no more than a piece of chalk.

A few years later, Charles' successor, King Louis XII, also had designs on Italy. Louis claimed that he had a hereditary right to the duchy of Milan through his relation to the Visconti family, who had ruled Milan prior to the Sforza family. Louis' interest in Italian territory coincided with the ambitions of the powerful Borgia family. Pope Alexander VI, born Rodrigo Borgia, wanted to make his son Cesare a force in Italy. To do so, he needed the help of the French armies. Louis, meanwhile, needed favors that only a pope could manage. In order to consolidate his position in France, Louis needed to marry Charles' widow, Anne of Brittany, but could not do so until his marriage to his current wife was annulled. He also wanted one of his advisors, Archbishop Georges d'Amboise, made a cardinal so that he would eventually be a candidate for the papacy. In exchange for these favors, Louis agreed to help Alexander and Cesare conquer the Romagna region and to undertake a campaign against the Kingdom of Naples, which both France and the pope had claims to. Louis was also urged on by the Venetians, who wanted revenge on Sforza and Milan. Louis invaded and captured Milan from Sforza in 1499. Many considered it poetic justice that Sforza had been deprived of his dukedom by the very forces he had first invited into Italy.

However, Louis' hold over Naples was weak. He initially installed a puppet ruler in Naples (his cousin, Frederick of Aragon), but made a secret arrangement to split the kingdom with King Ferdinand of Spain, who also claimed a hereditary right to Naples. Ferdinand quickly reneged on the agreement and drove the French forces out of Naples. Even so, the French still controlled much of Italy. Cesare Borgia may have threatened French power in Italy after his success in the Romagna region, but his father's sudden death left him without resources or influence.

After Alexander VI's successor, Pius III, died after less than a month in office, Cardinal Giuliano della Rovere became Pope Julius II in 1503. Julius earns several mentions in Machiavelli's narrative. As Machiavelli observes, he was every bit as warlike and ambitious as Alexander, but his goal was always to increase the power of the church, not to aggrandize his own family. Unlike Alexander, he was a good manager of money and resources and exercised restraint in his personal habits. He was also a wily politician.

In the power vacuum left after the collapse of Borgia power, Venice had seized part of the Romagna region, which traditionally belonged to the papacy, and they were also challenging Julius' authority in spiritual matters. In 1508, Julius formed the League of Cambrai, which included France, Spain, and the Holy Roman Empire, for the purpose of putting the Venetians back in their place. The Venetian armies were defeated at the battle of Agnadello (which Machiavelli refers to as Vailà) and Venice's conquered territories were lost. Soon after, Julius, who feared the French's hold over Italy, began working to get them out. During this period, Louis had Julius at his mercy on more than one occasion, but never pressed his advantage, a move that Machiavelli criticizes. Julius' efforts culminated in the formation of the Holy League, which included combined forces of the Venetians, the Holy Roman Empire, the Swiss, the English, and the Spanish. Despite a disastrous defeat at the battle of Ravenna, the League ultimately drove out Louis and his armies in 1512, putting him out of power in Italy. Machiavelli alludes to this fact in Chapter 3 of *The Prince* when he comments that it took the entire world to deprive Louis XII of his Italian conquests.

The Florentines had been longstanding allies of the French. The Soderini government supported Louis up until the bitter end and against all advice, even as the French were pulling out of Italy. Their loyalty left them at the mercy of Pope Julius and his Spanish allies, and this led directly to the fall of the Florentine republic which Machiavelli had served for so many years.

A Brief Synopsis

The Prince is an extended analysis of how to acquire and maintain political power. It includes 26 chapters and an opening dedication to Lorenzo de Medici. The dedication declares Machiavelli's intention to discuss in plain language the conduct of great men and the principles of princely government. He does so in hope of pleasing and enlightening the Medici family.

The book's 26 chapters can be divided into four sections: Chapters 1–11 discuss the different types of principalities or states, Chapters 12–14 discuss the different types of armies and the proper conduct of a prince as military leader, Chapters 15–23 discuss the character and behavior of the prince, and Chapters 24–26 discuss Italy's desperate political situation. The final chapter is a plea for the Medici family to supply the prince who will lead Italy out of humiliation.

The types of principalities

Machiavelli lists four types of principalities:

* Hereditary principalities, which are inherited by the ruler

* Mixed principalities, territories that are annexed to the ruler's existing territories

* New principalities, which may be acquired by several methods: by one's own power, by the power of others, by criminal acts or extreme cruelty, or by the will of the people (civic principalities)

* Ecclesiastical principalities, namely the Papal States belonging to the Catholic church

The types of armies

A prince must always pay close attention to military affairs if he wants to remain in power. Machiavelli lists four types of armies:

* Mercenaries or hired soldiers, which are dangerous and unreliable

* Auxiliaries, troops that are loaned to you by other rulers—also dangerous and unreliable

* Native troops, composed of one's own citizens or subjects—by far the most desirable kind

* Mixed troops, a combination of native troops and mercenaries or auxiliaries—still less desirable than a completely native army

The character and behavior of the prince

Machiavelli recommends the following character and behavior for princes:

* It is better to be stingy than generous.

* It is better to be cruel than merciful.

* It is better to break promises if keeping them would be against one's interests.

* Princes must avoid making themselves hated and despised; the goodwill of the people is a better defense than any fortress.

* Princes should undertake great projects to enhance their reputation.

* Princes should choose wise advisors and avoid flatterers.

Italy's political situation

Machiavelli outlines and recommends the following:

* The rulers of Italy have lost their states by ignoring the political and military principles Machiavelli enumerates.

* Fortune controls half of human affairs, but free will controls the rest, leaving the prince free to act. However, few princes can adapt their actions to the times.

* The final chapter is an exhortation to the Medici family to follow Machiavelli's principles and thereby free Italy from foreign domination.

List of Characters

Because *The Prince* is a political commentary, not a work of fiction, Machiavelli does not use "characters" in the sense of a novel or short story. Instead, he draws his examples from the current political and social events, as well as from ancient history. His "characters" are the political leaders of his time. He mentions far too many individuals to be listed here, but several make repeated appearances in *The Prince*, and it is helpful to keep them and their relationships in mind.

The Sforza family

Francesco Sforza Mercenary general who became Duke of Milan.

Ludovico Sforza Also called "Il Moro," the Moor. Son of Francesco Sforza and Duke of Milan, he encouraged King Charles VIII of France to invade Italy.

Caterina Sforza Riario Ludovico's niece, the illegitimate daughter of Gian Galeazzo Sforza. Ruler of the cities of Forli and Imola; called "The Amazon of Forli."

The Borgia family

Pope Alexander VI (Rodrigo Borgia) Corrupt and decadent leader of the church, who shamelessly maneuvered his many illegitimate children into positions of power.

Cesare Borgia Alexander VI's son, Duke of Valentinois in France, and conquerer of the Romagna region in Italy. Machiavelli's chief example of an ideal prince.

The Medici family, rulers of Florence

Lorenzo de Medici Grandson of Lorenzo the Magnificent. *The Prince* is dedicated to him.

Pope Leo X (Giovanni de Medici) Pope at the time *The Prince* was written. His election resulted in Machiavelli's release from prison.

Others

Pope Julius II Warrior pope who succeeded Alexander VI. Noted for his defense of the temporal and spiritual power of the Catholic church.

Girolamo Savonarola Charismatic preacher and prophet who ruled Florence after the Medici family was removed from power.

King Ferdinand Ruler of Spain. Better known to American students as the husband of Queen Isabella, who financed Christopher Columbus' voyages to the new world.

King Charles VIII Ruler of France who invaded Italy at the urging of Ludovico Sforza, but was quickly driven out.

King Louis XII Charles' successor. Invader of Italy and its main foreign dominator immediately prior to the time during which *The Prince* was written.

Emperor Maximilian II Ruler of the Holy Roman Empire, another European power with designs on Italy.

CRITICAL
COMMENTARIES

Dedication

Summary

Those who seek the favor of powerful men usually offer them precious material gifts, but Machiavelli instead offers his precious knowledge of the conduct of great men. He aims to present this knowledge in a plain and direct style. He observes that as a person of low social rank, he has the best perspective on the actions of those who are high above him, just as princes have the best perspective on the actions of the people. He hopes that his gracious patron will pity his humble and unfortunate position.

Commentary

Machiavelli addresses his book to Lorenzo de Medici, whom he calls magnificent, alluding to Lorenzo's famous grandfather, who was known as Lorenzo the Magnificent. Machiavelli had originally dedicated *The Prince* to Giuliano de Medici, one of Lorenzo the Magnificent's sons, but Giuliano died in 1516, and consequently would have been no help in putting Machiavelli back into political office. Machiavelli refers to his current miserable situation in the final paragraph.

Dedications to powerful patrons were attached to almost all works of Renaissance literature. They usually declared the author's unworthiness and praised the patron's greatness, and Machiavelli's dedication stands squarely in this tradition. However, he was sincere in his desire to get back into the good graces of the Medici family.

Machiavelli's plain manner of speaking can be found throughout the book. He discusses all his subjects, even the most shocking, in a cool and matter-of-fact tone, as if analyzing a scientific specimen.

Chapters 1 and 2

Summary

There are two types of states: republics and principalities. Machiavelli declares that he will not discuss republics, examining only how principalities may be acquired and governed. Principalities are inherited or new.

New principalities are either annexed to a ruler's existing territory or are completely new. New principalities are either used to being ruled by a prince or are used to being free. New principalities are acquired by luck or by strength.

Hereditary principalities, which are used to being ruled by the prince's family, are easy to maintain, because tradition keeps the prince's position stable as long as he does not make himself hated.

Commentary

Theme

In Chapter 1, Machiavelli traces the basic outlines of a discussion that will take him through Chapter 11: the different types of states, how to acquire them, and the difficulties they present to a ruler. Machiavelli refers to republics, which are governed by their citizens, and principalities or princely states, which are governed by a single, strong ruler (a prince). Because he is addressing one of those princes, he avoids any discussion of republican government, except to note that republics conquered by a new prince are used to living free, a theme he returns to in later chapters. In many of his other works, Machiavelli passionately defended republican forms of government, and he suffered for his defense of the Florentine republic which the Medici now ruled.

Character Insight

Hereditary principalities are those in which rule is passed down among members of one family. Machiavelli considers these the easiest to govern and therefore disposes of the subject by observing that any minimally competent prince can hold onto one. At the end of Chapter 2, Machiavelli makes the first of his many observations about human nature, noting that people are inclined to forget that even old established governments were innovations once.

Glossary

(Here and in the following chapters, allusions and historical references are explained.)

Milan/Sforza Francesco Sforza (1401–1466) became Duke of Milan in 1450. (See the List of Characters.)

Naples/King of Spain Ferdinand (1452–1516) had originally agreed to divide the Italian kingdom of Naples with Louis XII of France, but Ferdinand drove out the French forces and took over Naples in 1503.

Duke of Ferrara actually two dukes, Ercole d'Este (1431–1505), who lost territory to the Venetians in 1484, and his successor, Alfonso d'Este (1476–1534), who managed to stay in power despite the opposition of three different popes. The d'Este family had ruled Ferrara for almost four centuries.

Chapter 3

Summary

New principalities always cause problems for the prince. People are willing to change rulers to better their own lot, but they soon discover that things have gotten worse, because a new ruler must harm those he conquers. Then you have as enemies those you harmed while seizing power, as well as those who put you in power, because you can never satisfy all of their ambitions.

If conquered territories annexed to yours are similar in location and customs, it is easy to keep them, especially if they were hereditary principalities not used to independence. As long as you do not change their way of life, you need only wipe out the old ruling family to keep them.

But if new territories are different in language and customs, they are difficult to keep. The best methods are to go and live there yourself, to establish colonies in them, to protect the neighboring minor powers, to weaken strong factions within the state, and to guard against foreign powers. It is important to deal with developing political problems early, rather than wait until it is too late, because wars can never be avoided, only postponed. King Louis did not follow these policies in Italy and therefore failed to keep his territories. He also erred by making the Church more powerful, because to make others powerful is to weaken yourself.

Commentary

In this long chapter about annexed territories, Machiavelli makes several of the observations that have contributed to his reputation for ruthlessness. First, he notes that conquering rulers must inevitably injure those they conquer. Then he advises conquerors to exterminate old ruling families to avoid threats to their power. Discussing colonies, he says they are effective because the only ones they harm are a few poor people who lose their homes and lands, and these people are in no position to harm the prince. In this context, he makes the famous statement that men should either be caressed or destroyed, meaning that if you must harm people, harm them so severely that they will not be able to take revenge on you.

Other pieces of Machiavelli's advice seem more humane. He justifies colonies as an effective means to control a new territory because they harm the minimum number of people, and it is impossible for a new ruler to avoid doing some harm to his subjects. Colonies are definitely more desirable than occupation by an army, which harms everyone in the new state and makes the new ruler hated. While he sees violence as an unavoidable part of government, he strives for the most efficient and controlled use of violence. Yet readers may object that Machiavelli advises the prince to act humanely only when doing so has a tangible benefit, not because doing so is ethical. Machiavelli's advice to the prince is always grounded in the best way to acquire and increase power, rather than in considerations of right or wrong. Power is depicted as a scarce resource to be energetically collected and carefully guarded, as in Machiavelli's observation that giving power to another takes power from yourself. This intensely competitive outlook precludes ideas of cooperation or shared responsibility. Much of this chapter is concerned with detailed analysis of the examples provided by the Romans in ancient times and King Louis in more recent times. Louis's invasion was the beginning of a turbulent period for Italy, and its repercussions occupy Machiavelli's attention later in the book.

Glossary

Ludovico Ludovico Sforza (1451–1508), Duke of Milan and son of Francesco Sforza. (See the List of Characters.)

Turks/Greece Forces of the Ottoman Empire (the Turks) controlled Greece and much of the Balkan peninsula in the 15th century and followed a policy of settling in their conquered territories.

Aetolians The Aetolians and Achaeans were rival confederacies of Greek states. In circa 211 B.C., the Aetolians asked the Romans to help them fight against Philip V of Macedon. The Romans defeated Philip and, a few years later, defeated the Aetolians and their new ally, Antiochus III of Syria, effectively taking over Greece.

King Louis Louis XII (1462–1515), King of France. (See the List of Characters.)

Chapters 4 and 5

Summary

All principalities are governed either by a single ruler assisted by his appointed ministers or by a ruler and the hereditary nobles who hold power in their own right and have the loyalty of their subjects.

The Turkish sultan divides his kingdom into districts that are managed by his administrators, but the king of France has to contend with many lords who have longstanding privileges. Because the sultan's administrators are dependent on him for their power, they are not likely to help a foreign invader. But if an invader had a strong enough army to win, it would be easy to keep their territory, because the people are not personally loyal to the administrators. In a kingdom like France, the nobles are always ambitious and ready to turn against the king. But if they assist you in conquering the country, they will also be ready to turn on you. Even if you kill all the royal family, the nobles remain, and you can neither satisfy them nor get rid of them. Whether one can control a territory depends less on personal ability than on the character of the territory.

If the conquered territory was formerly a republic, in which the citizens were used to living under their own laws, you must destroy it, go live in it, or let the citizens live under their own laws with a government that is friendly to you. If you do not destroy the city, it will destroy you, so fiercely will the citizens remember and long for their freedom.

Commentary

Machiavelli contrasts two types of government: a strongly centralized model, which he identifies with the East, and the looser confederated model that dominated in Western Europe. Machiavelli had ample opportunities to see the kinds of internal problems that afflicted decentralized collections of states. The example he cites, France, was actually remarkably stable and unified in comparison with his own region of Italy, where competing states invited foreign powers to invade, then turned on them, only to turn on each other as soon as the threat passed.

Italy had indeed proved almost impossible to conquer, for exactly the reasons Machiavelli cites, but it had also proved impossible to unify.

Machiavelli's comments about governing a conquered republic sound especially merciless: destroy it, he cautions, or it will certainly destroy you. However, if you read Machiavelli's advice as directed toward the new Medici rulers of Florence, it takes on a different tone. If you want to avoid being destroyed by it, you must come and live in it and rule it directly, he says. This is exactly what the Medici had failed to do in the period since their return to power, spending almost all their time away from Florence. Machiavelli's vivid portrayal of the republic's love of liberty can be read as a kind of warning to the Medici about how ready their new possession will be to return to its republican ways if they do not do more to govern it.

Theme

In Chapter 4, Machiavelli begins elaborating on the theme of ability versus circumstances in determining a leader's success or failure. He implies that the leader's talents are less important than the situation he finds himself in. Machiavelli discusses this theme in detail throughout the book, culminating in his statements about fortune and free will in Chapter 25. The contrast between luck, specifically the favor of others, and ability is further explained in Chapters 6 and 7.

Glossary

Alexander Alexander the Great (356–323 B.C.), King of Macedon and one of the great conquerors of the ancient world.

Darius (circa 380–330 B.C.) King of Persia, one of the territories that Alexander conquered.

Pyrrhus King of Epirus who fought against the Romans. He won several victories, but at a very high price.

Pisa In 1406, Florence bought the city of Pisa from the dukes of Milan; in 1494, when Charles VII invaded, the Pisans asserted their liberty from Florence. Florence won Pisa back in 1509.

Chapter 6

Summary

The difficulty a new prince will have will depend on his ability. Private citizens become princes either through luck or through ability, but it is best not to trust luck. Those who become prince through their own strength have difficulty gaining power, but keep it easily. Establishing new states is always troublesome, because everyone who was happy under the old order will oppose change, and most people will not support new things until they have seen them work.

The question is whether innovators must rely on others in order to succeed, or whether they can rely on their own forces. Armed prophets succeed, but unarmed prophets must fail. The people are fickle, and when they no longer believe in you, you must force them to believe.

Commentary

Theme

Chapter 6 elaborates on a theme begun in Chapter 5—that of personal ability. The Italian word Machiavelli uses is *virtù*, which does not have an exact English equivalent. He uses this word to mean many things, but usually not "virtue," which in English implies goodness and moral behavior. *Virtù* is closer in meaning to the Latin word for masculine strength, *virtus*, from which English gets the word "virility." Exactly what Machiavelli means by *virtù* is a subject of debate among scholars. *Virtù* can be ability, skill, energy, forcefulness, strength, ingenuity, courage, or determination. *Virtù* is the quality that distinguishes successful princes—or more accurately, successful innovators and conquerors. The examples Machiavelli provides are all legendary founders of great civilizations. When they found opportunities, they had the *virtù* to make the most of them. Machiavelli makes a point of observing, however, that *virtù* without opportunity to use it is wasted, but without *virtù*, opportunity is wasted.

Theme

The other theme of this chapter concerns the use of force. Machiavelli assumes that force or violence is an integral part of the state, and a ruler cannot do without it as a tool of government. He observes that after your followers lose faith in your innovative schemes, you must force them to have faith, or at least, to act as if they do by obeying you. His comment about unarmed prophets is based on the meteoric rise and fall of Savonarola, whose career Machiavelli had observed, and whose failure had led to the reestablishment of the Florentine republic in which Machiavelli served.

Glossary

Moses prophet and lawgiver who led the Israelites out of captivity in Egypt, as recounted in the Biblical book of Exodus.

Cyrus "the Great," founder of the Persian Empire, beginning with his conquest of the Medes (circa 549 B.C.).

Romulus with his brother Remus, the legendary founders of Rome.

Theseus legendary hero of Athens who killed the Minotaur, a half-man, half-bull monster, in the Labyrinth of Crete.

Savonarola Girolamo Savonarola (1452–1498). Dominican monk, charismatic preacher, and reformer. (See the List of Characters.)

Hiero also called Hieron II, King of Syracuse (circa 271-216 B.C.). He was made commander of the Syracusan army and was so successful that he was elected king by the citizens.

Chapter 7

Summary

Citizens who become princes through luck or the favor of others find it easy to acquire their states, but difficult to keep them. They are not used to being in command, and they have no armies of their own.

Francesco Sforza became a prince by his own strength and kept his state. Cesare Borgia became a prince by his father's influence, and, despite his best efforts, could not maintain his state after his father's influence failed. This was not his fault, but was caused by extraordinary bad luck. Alexander VI wanted to make his son great, but had no troops he could rely on. Alexander allowed the French into Italy in exchange for the use of their troops to conquer the Romagna region. Borgia succeeded and made more conquests, but worried about the French king and the loyalty of his Roman troops, led by the Orsini family. He lured the Orsini leaders with gifts and promises of friendship, then killed them all. He won the loyalty of the people in Romagna. He had at first found the Romagna to be lawless, so he put Remirro de Orco in charge of restoring order, which he did well. However, Remirro de Orco was so cruel that everyone hated him, so to deflect bad feeling from himself, Borgia had him publicly executed.

At this point Borgia had laid good foundations for his power. But abruptly Alexander died, and Borgia himself was extremely ill. Borgia then made a mistake by not preventing the election of a Pope hostile to him. In short, Borgia was a model prince and did all things well, except for his poor judgment about Julius II, which caused his downfall.

Commentary

Although Machiavelli offers an example of a prince who rose to power through his own ability in Francesco Sforza, he devotes most of this long chapter to the analysis of the career of Cesare Borgia, whose rise depended on the favor of others, namely his powerful father, Pope Alexander VI (born Rodrigo Borgia). Machiavelli's admiration for

Borgia shines throughout the description. He sees in Borgia a model for all princely conquerors. Machiavelli had an opportunity to personally observe this dynamic Duke when he was sent by the Florentine council to negotiate with Borgia about relations with Florence. Machiavelli was on this mission when Borgia lured his enemies to the city of Senigallia and had them strangled, and Machiavelli spoke with Borgia about the incident. Borgia was by all accounts ruthless, ambitious, and boundlessly energetic, possessing a forceful personality that impressed those around him. It is no accident that these are the same qualities possessed by Machiavelli's ideal prince.

Borgia radiates *virtù*, but in the end it is not enough to save him, because he remains dependent on the power and influence of his father. Pure bad luck—his father's sudden death and his own unexpected illness—puts him on the path to ruin. The dangers of dependency on others will become a key point in Machiavelli's arguments, one he emphasizes later in his discussion of armies.

Machiavelli's endorsement of Borgia's tactics, including deceit, brutality, and betrayal of his own agents, is enthusiastic. One may be more inclined to judge Borgia as a heartless master manipulator, expertly playing factions against one another, using those around him as needed and disposing of them as they become inconvenient. But for a brief period, he was stunningly successful, on the verge of consolidating his hold over Italy—and success in controlling the state is all that matters in Machiavelli's analysis. He will be more explicit in Chapter 18 on how necessary it is for a prince to be deceitful when circumstances call for it, and in Chapter 17 how cruelty is often better than mercy to preserve the peace and order of the state.

Glossary

Duke Valentino Cesare Borgia was often referred to as Duke Valentino or Duke Valentinois, a title he was granted by Louis XII of France.

Orsini and Colonna rival families of the Roman aristocracy, both enormously powerful in Italian politics. The Orsini family, in particular, was a bitter opponent of the Borgias, and Cesare Borgia ordered at least three of the leading Orsini family members to be killed.

College of Cardinals an assembly that is responsible for electing a successor when a Pope dies.

San Piero Machiavelli refers to a number of cardinals (Colonna, San Giorgio, Ascanio, and Rouen) who were potential candidates for Pope, calling some of them by the names of their churches. "San Piero" was Giuliano della Rovere, who become Pope Julius II. "Rouen," whom Machiavelli thinks Borgia should have contrived to elect, was Georges d'Amboise.

Chapter 8

Summary

Theme

Continuing his theme from Chapter 7, Machiavelli discusses two other ways to becoming a prince: by criminal means or when private citizens choose a ruler from their fellow citizens. Machiavelli declines to discuss the first method at length, because it speaks for itself. Agathocles was wicked, but through his great energy became a military commander in Syracuse. In order to become ruler, he called the Senate and the leading citizens together for a meeting, and then massacred them. His ability made him a prince, but such conduct cannot be called virtuous. One can get power this way, but not glory. For example, Oliverotto of Fermo became a military commander and plotted with a few leading citizens to take over the city. His uncle arranged a lavish banquet to welcome him. On a prearranged signal, Oliverotto and his soldiers killed all the guests, including his uncle, and then terrorized the city into obedience. He was only removed from power when Cesare Borgia had him murdered at Senigallia.

Cruel acts, though evil, may be justified when they are done all at once to establish a prince's power (but not repeated) and turned to the benefit of his subjects. Cruel acts are done badly when they increase over time. A conqueror should decide how many injuries he must inflict up front and do them all at once to keep his subjects from constantly resenting them. But benefits should be handed out gradually, so that people savor them. Above all, a prince should live with his subjects in such a way that no good or bad situation can force him to change his conduct.

Commentary

Many readers have found evidence in this chapter and the previous one for Machiavelli's approval of vicious behavior. Clearly, Machiavelli admires the energy and ability (*virtù*) of men like Agathocles, but he is careful to qualify his approval. He says that it cannot be called "virtue" (and here he uses the same word, *virtù*) for a prince to be devoid of conscience. Criminal acts may give a prince power, but they cannot place him among the truly great rulers of history, whose acts are to be admired and imitated. However, it is difficult to reconcile Machiavelli's criticism of Agathocles and Oliverotto with his glowing admiration of Cesare Borgia, particularly when all three employed the same tactic of inviting their opponents to a supposedly friendly setting and then murdering them. Oliverotto, in fact, foolishly fell for this ploy after using it himself, having been betrayed by a better betrayer, namely Borgia.

At this point in the argument, Machiavelli the moralist steps away, and Machiavelli the coolly rational observer of politics returns. How is it, he asks, that criminals like this stay securely in power when many leaders who have done much less evil cannot keep their positions? He replies that even evil acts may be put to good use if they are handled properly. Evils done in the beginning, to secure the new state and to establish orderly government and not made into a habit may be excusable, even in Agathocles' case—a striking observation, because Machiavelli had previously called him devoid of truth, pity, or religion. This may explain why he can approve of Borgia but nominally condemn Agathocles and Oliverotto: He views Borgia as a bringer of order and unity to a divided and suffering Italy. As long as evils are turned as quickly as possible to benefits for one's subjects, they can be forgiven, because, as Machiavelli has already observed, it is impossible for conquerors to avoid injuring some of their subjects at first. There are other practical reasons to avoid terrorizing one's subjects, for if a prince abuses them constantly, he will never be able to rely on their support, a point to which Machiavelli returns in the next chapter.

While Machiavelli does not exactly advocate criminal acts, neither does he oppose them, as long as they achieve the desired goal. If one chooses not to call this stance immoral, it is at least amoral; that is, not concerned with the moral value of an action. The philosophy of "the end justifies the means" has often been associated with Machiavelli and is easily subject to abuses in the name of progress.

Glossary

Agathocles (circa 361–289 B.C.), King of Syracuse. Exiled from Syracuse because of his power and popularity, he was able to return through the intervention of Hamilcar, leader of the Syracusan's allies, the Carthaginians. A military coup followed in which

Agathocles killed or banished the oligarchy that had ruled the city. Machiavelli summarizes Agathocles' long campaigns against the Carthaginians.

Oliverotto da Fermo (circa 1475–1503). Machiavelli accurately describes how he seized power. Soon after, he joined a conspiracy of Cesare Borgia's captains to try to limit Borgia's growing power. This group included Vitellozzo Vitelli, the brother of Oliverotto's mentor, Paolo Vitelli. Pretending to be reconciled with them, Borgia lured the conspirators to a meeting at Senigallia, where he had them killed.

Chapter 9

Summary

When private citizens become rulers through the favor of their fellow citizens, these may be called *civil principalities*. One can reach this position through the favor of either the common citizens or the nobles, because the two classes are found in every city. The nobles want only to oppress the people, and the people want only to avoid oppression. From these opposing impulses can come three results: a principality, a republic, or anarchy. When the nobles feel pressure from the people, they try to make one of their own the prince in order to protect their privileges. When the people feel they cannot resist the nobles, they try to make a fellow citizen prince in order to protect their rights. You can never satisfy the nobles by acting honorably, but you can satisfy the people.

Regardless of how a prince comes to power, he should make every effort to win the good will of the people, or in times of trouble, he will have no hope. A prince must not delude himself about the reliability of the people, but nonetheless, a prince who makes good preparations and knows how to command will never be betrayed by them. A wise ruler will contrive to keep all his citizens dependent on him and on the state, and then he will be able to trust them.

Commentary

Theme

Machiavelli's theme in this chapter is the relationship between the people (the ordinary citizens) and their opposites, the nobles (the upper classes from aristocratic families). Machiavelli portrays these two groups as constantly at odds, but his sympathy is clearly with the people, who only want to live free under the rule of their own laws. Machiavelli himself belonged firmly in this group, having been prevented from holding high office because he was not an aristocrat, and having served his entire career in Florence's civil government. The Medici, to whom he was writing, were members of the nobility, and this makes his advice somewhat more daring than it may sound at first. As in Chapter 5, Machiavelli can be seen reminding the Medici how much free states like Florence value their freedom and how justified they are in doing so.

Machiavelli emphasizes how necessary it is for a prince to win over the people, because they are many, while the nobles are few, and a prince can never live safely without being able to trust the people. On this subject, Machiavelli was going against prevailing opinion, which he acknowledges by quoting the proverb "He who builds on the people builds on mud." In fact, he is able to find only one example to support his argument (Nabis the Spartan), but two that disprove it (the Gracchi and Messer Scali). Machiavelli had many opportunities to observe the fickleness of the Florentine people, as they had alternately supported the Medici, Savonarola, the Republic, and then the Medici again.

In another pessimistic observation about human nature, Machiavelli says that everyone is ready to die for you when the prospect of death is far off. The key, he maintains, is for the prince to keep his subjects dependent on him for all their benefits, because dependency is the only way to ensure loyalty. Characteristically, Machiavelli advocates a particular behavior not for its moral qualities, but because it accomplishes a specific goal for the prince: A prince should treat his subjects well and do all he can to benefit them, not necessarily because it is right to do so, but because it ultimately consolidates the prince's power.

Theme

Machiavelli also insists on the importance of self-interest as a motivator throughout the chapter: He notes that all parties, whether princes, nobles, or common people, come into conflict or make alliances primarily to protect their own rights and privileges. Throughout the book, self-interest and a concern for one's own comfort level can be seen as the driving force in human behavior.

Glossary

Nabis ruler of Sparta (circa 207–192 B.C.). Machiavelli is probably exaggerating Nabis' success, but Nabis did introduce many social reforms.

Gracchi brothers Tiberius (166–133 B.C.) and Gaius Gracchus (154–121 B.C.). Roman officials who instituted many social reforms and were killed by aristocratic opponents.

Giorgio Scali a leader of the Ciompi (wool workers) revolt in Florence in 1378. The wool workers' guild briefly held some political power, but its leaders, including Scali, were quickly overthrown and later executed.

Chapter 10

Summary

One other measure of a state's strength is whether a prince can defend himself, or whether he must rely on the help of others. If a ruler can field his own army (either his own men or paid mercenaries), he needs no outside help, but if he must hide behind his city walls, he will always need help from others. The first type has already been discussed in Chapter 6, and will be again in Chapters 12 through 14. The second type has no option but to fortify his city and lay in supplies. If he has treated his subjects well and has made preparations, others will hesitate to attack him. The free German cities follow this practice with great success. Therefore, any prince who has a strong city and has not made his people hate him is safe. Some will argue that the stresses of a siege will make the people disloyal, but a wise ruler will know how to keep up their morale, as long as there are enough weapons and supplies.

Commentary

Winning the people's support is absolutely necessary if a prince faces the possibility of a siege. Sieges were commonplace in medieval and Renaissance warfare, and many medieval cities were surrounded by high walls in anticipation of just such an event. Sieges were often lengthy affairs, with the attacking army camped outside the city walls, hoping to starve out or wear down the residents inside the city's fortifications. As Machiavelli observes, a prince in this position could only wait out the siege or hope for outside help. Machiavelli considers it better for the prince to have an army he can put into the field on the offensive, so that the prince need not be dependent on the favor of others. However, a prince with a strong and loyal city is still in a good position, as long as he has made adequate preparations and keeps his people's spirits up. Finally, he gives some attention to the prince's ability to "spin" political events to his advantage; in this case, to reassure his people that the siege will be short, to remind them of the cruelty of the enemy, and to take measures to deal with anyone who is a little too outspoken in his criticism of the prince's policies.

Theme

The absolute necessity of maintaining one's own troops is a point Machiavelli revisits throughout the book, and particularly in Chapters 12 through 14, which concern how a prince should behave in military matters. Machiavelli had been active in raising a native militia to defend Florence, and he detested the common practice of hiring foreign mercenaries to fight, a practice he believed had helped to ruin Italy. Here, he praises the independence of the German cities, which had their own armies to fight for them.

Glossary

German cities the Holy Roman Empire, a loose confederacy of states that comprised most of what is now Germany, as well as parts of Italy and France. In Machiavelli's time, the empire included more than 70 imperial cities, which exercised greater and lesser degrees of obedience to the Emperor, Maximilian I.

Chapter 11

Summary

The final type of principality to be discussed is the ecclesiastical state. Although this type of principality is gained through ability or luck, their princes stay in power no matter how they act. They do not defend their states or govern their people, and the people never think of getting rid of them. No other state could be so successful. Because these states are ordained by God, Machiavelli says he will not be so foolish as to discuss them.

Still, some people may ask how these states became so powerful so quickly. Before Charles invaded Italy, it was controlled by five factions whose goals were to keep out foreign invaders and make sure no one faction became too strong. The short reign of most popes kept them from making any headway against these factions. Then Alexander VI appeared, and he showed what a Pope could accomplish with money and weapons. Though he wanted only to promote Cesare Borgia's power, he ended up making the Church more powerful, which Julius II took advantage of. One hopes that the present Pope Leo will make it as great by his goodness as others have made it by force.

Commentary

In this chapter, Machiavelli completes his discussion of the different kinds of states and how to acquire them, which he laid out in Chapter 1. The *ecclesiastical states* he refers to were a unique feature of the Italian political landscape, namely the Papal States. As he notes, they followed none of the rules that would have applied to other kinds of principalities. The popes, as head of the Catholic church, which was arguably the most powerful institution in Europe, had always had power and privilege, and had ruled over their own states around Rome. But the popes of the Italian Renaissance added military conquest and aggressive fund-raising to the mix, becoming not only outrageously powerful but outrageously corrupt as well. The abuses of Alexander VI—who had children by several mistresses, lived a decadent lifestyle, and undertook military campaigns to aggrandize his family—played a significant part in bringing about the backlash of the Protestant Reformation. The collecting of indulgences, a practice Martin Luther protested strongly, was one of the chief sources of income for Alexander's military ventures.

Style & Language

Machiavelli's comment that he cannot presume to discuss a state ordained by God fairly drips with sarcasm. Machiavelli was well aware of the thoroughly worldly ambitions of the Renaissance popes and bitterly resented their effect on Italian politics. In his *Discourses on Livy*, he has harsh words for the Church's lack of religious principle and willingness to promote factionalism in Italy, depriving it of a strong, centralized leadership such as existed in France and Spain.

Glossary

Pope Leo X Giovanni de Medici (1475–1521). A son of Lorenzo the Magnificent, and therefore uncle of the man to whom *The Prince* was dedicated. He became Pope in 1513. It was during the general amnesty celebrating his election that Machiavelli had been released from prison. Leo would later excommunicate Martin Luther, the Protestant reformer.

Chapter 12

Summary

Having discussed the different types of states in Chapters 2 through 11, Machiavelli now turns to how to attack and defend them. Princes must lay good foundations, and those foundations include good laws and good armies. There cannot be good laws without good armies, and where there are good laws, there must be good arms, so Machiavelli declares he will only discuss arms, not laws.

Arms to defend the state are the prince's own, mercenaries, auxiliaries, or a mix of the three. Mercenaries and auxiliaries are dangerous and unreliable. If a mercenary is talented, he will always be trying to increase his power at the prince's expense. If he is incompetent, he will ruin the prince. Only princes and republics that can field their own armies can succeed, for mercenaries do nothing but lose. Those who are well armed can live free.

Machiavelli cites many examples of mercenaries who have turned on their employers. All this began when the Holy Roman Empire lost power in Italy and the popes gained power. Citizens took up arms against the nobles, and the popes encouraged them. Because neither the citizens nor the popes knew how to fight, they hired mercenaries. Soon mercenaries commanded every army in Italy. These mercenaries adopted strategies that kept them from hard work and danger, and this caused the ruin and humiliation of Italy.

Commentary

Theme

This chapter and the two following concern arms and armies. It is tempting to interpret Machiavelli's quotable line that there cannot be good laws without good arms as just a variation on "might makes right," but this was probably not his intent. Because force is an inseparable part of the state, a well-governed state needs a good army. If the reader interprets "good laws" not in the strict legal sense, but as the conditions that make for orderly life in society, Machiavelli's observation loses some of its radical edge. Even in the modern world, the state that does not rely on police or military force to keep order and protect its citizens is rare indeed. Machiavelli further observes that where there are good arms there must be good laws, meaning that a ruler who is capable enough to raise and command a disciplined army must also be capable enough to keep his state well ordered.

Literary Device

Equally important is what Machiavelli chooses *not* to discuss. Just as in Chapter 1, where he declined to discuss republics, here he declines to discuss laws, confining himself to a prince's command of the military. However, the world he describes is clearly one of cutthroat competition and violence, in which only the well armed can live free. In such a world, the weak will quickly be exploited by the strong unless they can defend themselves.

"Good arms," in Machiavelli's view, can be only the state's own troops; that is, its own citizens, rather than outsiders. Keeping with his view that independence and self-sufficiency are the only security, Machiavelli asserts that dependence on foreign troops is the kiss of death to a prince's power. He had good reasons to think so, having observed the widespread use of foreign mercenaries in Italy and what he felt were its disastrous consequences. He blamed the mercenaries for lacking the spirit of soldiers who were defending their own lands and homes. In his opinion, the mercenaries were lazy, looking only for the easiest way to get their money, regardless of whether this benefited the state that employed them. They were also untrustworthy, because if they worked for a prince's money, they were probably just as willing to work for the prince's opponent.

Theme

Notice also Machiavelli's characteristic assessment of human selfishness: If you hire a talented mercenary who is successful, you will never be safe, because he will want to take over your position.

Mercenaries were common in the Renaissance. Ironically, the most famous were the Italian *condottieri*, sophisticated professional soldiers who spent their lives serving various employers. Criticism of them was commonplace and not necessarily always deserved, because many of them were highly successful and loyal to their employers' interests. Both foreign and Italian mercenaries participated in Italian warfare.

Glossary

chalk Alexander VI supposedly remarked that Charles VIII of France was able to conquer Italy with a piece of chalk, simply by marking the doors of houses in order to claim them as quarters for his soldiers.

sins Savonarola interpreted the foreign invasions as punishment for Italian sinfulness, but Machiavelli says that the only sin involved was that of relying on mercenaries.

Carthage ancient city-state in northern Africa, founded by Phoenician near the site of modern Tunis and destroyed by Romans, rebuilt by Romans, and destroyed by Arabs.

Epaminondas a famous Theban general. Philip II of Macedon (382–336 B.C.) was not a mercenary but an ally of the Thebans.

Duke Filippo Filippo Maria Visconti (1392–1447), Duke of Milan. Francesco Sforza's rise to power in Milan is described in Chapter 2.

Queen Giovanna Giovanna II of Naples (1371–1435). The incident referred to involved a dispute between Giovanna and Muzio Attendolo Sforza (1369–1424). Sforza supported Louis III of Anjou as Giovanna's successor, while she favored Alfonso V, King of Aragon.

John Hawkwood (circa 1320–1394), also called Giovanni Acuto, an English mercenary who spent his career in Italy. Near the end of his life, he worked for the Florentines.

Paolo Vitelli (circa 1459–1499) mercenary leader employed by the Florentines. The Florentine government became suspicious of his conduct in the war against Pisa and had him executed.

Carmagnola Francesco Bussone (1380–1432), Count of Caramagnola, was a mercenary originally employed by the Milanese and dismissed by them. He was then employed by the Venetians, for whom he defeated the Milanese army. The Venetians were suspicious of his relationship with the Milanese and had him executed.

Vailà the city at which the League of Cambrai, including forces of Julius II and Louis XII, defeated the Venetians in 1509.

Empire the Holy Roman Empire, in west-central Europe, comprising the German-speaking peoples and northern Italy.

Alberigo da Cunio Alberigo da Barbiano (1348–1409), Count of Cunio. He founded the Company of St. George, the first company of Italian mercenaries.

Chapter 13

Summary

Auxiliaries are troops sent by another ruler to help you. Just as with mercenaries, if they lose, you are ruined, and if they win, you are in their power. Auxiliaries come to you as a united body trained to obey others. Mercenaries are less dangerous, because they are not united behind their leaders. A wise prince would rather lose his own troops than win with someone else's, because a victory with borrowed troops is not really a victory.

A principality that does not have its own army is not really secure, because it depends on fortune, not its own strength. Nothing is weaker than a reputation for power that is not based on your own strength.

Commentary

Machiavelli views auxiliaries, troops loaned by another ruler, as even more destructive than mercenaries. While mercenaries are only self-interested, auxiliaries are actually loyal to someone else, namely a rival prince who may use them to conquer you. Using forces that belong to someone else puts you in that person's power.

Returning once again to his theme that the only real strength is self-sufficiency, Machiavelli remarks that it is better to lose with one's own troops than to win with the strength of others, because that victory belongs to them. Unless a prince can field an army of his own citizens or subjects, he has no real power. *Virtù*, a prince's own strength, is always preferable to relying on luck or the favor of others.

Glossary

Julius Pope Julius II tried to take Ferrara, allied with the French, in 1510. Julius probably allied with Spain more out of fear of French power in Italy than out of specific desire to conquer Ferrara.

Constantinople former name for Istanbul. Christian capital of the Byzantine Empire. During a period of civil war, the emperor asked Ottoman Turkish forces to intervene. Constantinople fell to the Ottoman Empire in 1453.

David the great king of the Israelites, only a young shepherd boy when he fought for King Saul against the Philistine giant, Goliath. David's refusal of Saul's armor appears in I Samuel 17:38–40.

Charles VIII (1403–1461) King of France. His royal ordinances established permanent infantry and cavalry in the French army. His successor Louis XII reversed this policy.

Goths Germanic people who invaded and conquered most of the Roman Empire.

Chapter 14

Summary

The study of war should be a prince's main goal, for war is a ruler's only art. Knowledge of war is so vital that it not only keeps princes in power but can make princes out of private citizens. If princes become too refined to study this art, they lose their states.

Being unarmed makes others contemptuous of you. No one can expect an armed man to obey an unarmed one. Therefore a prince who does not understand military matters will not be able to work well with his soldiers. Even in peacetime, a prince must concentrate on war by exercises and by study. Hunting is excellent exercise, because it strengthens the body and makes the prince more familiar with the surrounding terrain. A prince should always be asking himself how to make the best military advantage of the landscape.

A prince should also exercise his mind by reading the histories of great men and how they waged war, in order to imitate them. Great leaders have always tried to emulate the qualities of those worthy examples who preceded them. By studying their precepts in good times, the prince will be ready when fortune changes.

Commentary

Chapter 14 marks the end of Machiavelli's discussion of armies and the beginning of his exploration of the prince's character. Before leaving the topic of armies, Machiavelli has some parting comments for those princes who become too soft to tend to military matters. The Sforzas were uppermost in Machiavelli's mind in this respect, having gone from commoners to dukes in only one generation because of their skills as mercenary soldiers, only to go from dukes to commoners in the next generation. This observation is sometimes interpreted as a warning to the Medici family, who were notable for their lack of military leadership. Unlike most Italian princes of their day, they relied on their wealth and their diplomatic skills, rather than weapons, to secure their power. Military prowess was a very real way to get to the top in Machiavelli's day. In the cutthroat world of Italian politics, an unarmed prince would quickly be undone by his more rapacious neighbors. More importantly, Machiavelli argues for carrying a big stick, because no one can expect an unarmed man to command one who is armed.

Machiavelli recommends both physical and mental discipline to keep the prince sharp. Hunting was one of the favorite pastimes of the Middle Ages and Renaissance and was widely recommended as good exercise. Machiavelli also sees it as an opportunity for reconnaissance. While he may be exaggerating somewhat, he makes the point he first made in Chapter 3, that the prince must always be thinking about future events and preparing for potential problems. Mental exercise involved studying history. The humanist scholars of the Renaissance deeply valued the study of history, particularly the histories of classical Greece and Rome, and the imitation of their precepts. In this humanist tradition, Machiavelli draws many of his examples from classical history, blending them with lessons from contemporary events. He closes the chapter with a discussion of personal qualities of the great leaders of history. This leads him into the theme of the next segment of the book, the behavior and character of the prince.

Glossary

Philopoemen (253–184 B.C.) Greek general and leader of the Achaean League; he defeated Nabis the Spartan on several occasions.

Alexander Alexander the Great. Machiavelli proposes that Alexander imitated the example of Achilles, the legendary Greek warrior who appears in Homer's Iliad; Julius Caesar (100–44 B.C.), the great Roman general and emperor, imitated Alexander; and Scipio Africanus (circa 236–183 B.C.), another great Roman general, imitated Cyrus the Great, the founder of the Persian empire.

Xenophon author of the *Cyropaedia*, purportedly a biography of Cyrus the Great, but actually an exploration of how an ideal ruler should be educated.

Chapter 15

Summary

The proper behavior of princes toward subjects and allies remains to be discussed. Many others have treated this subject, but Machiavelli bases his observations on the real world, not on an imagined ideal. There is so much difference between the way people should act and the way they do act that any prince who tries to do what he should will ruin himself. A prince must know when to act immorally. Everyone agrees that a prince should have all good qualities, but because that is impossible, a wise prince will avoid those vices that would destroy his power and not worry about the rest. Some actions that seem virtuous will ruin a prince, while others that seem like vices will make a prince prosper.

Commentary

Theme

In this chapter, Machiavelli introduces the theme that will occupy much of the rest of the book: how princes should act. He announces his intention to turn the reader's expectations upside down by recommending that princes be bad rather than good. He was consciously going against a long tradition of advice books for rulers, the "Mirror for Princes" genre, which predictably recommended that leaders be models of virtue, always upholding the highest moral standards and being honest, trustworthy, generous, and merciful. Machiavelli declares that this is fine if you are an imaginary model prince living in a perfect world, but in the real world, a prince is surrounded by unscrupulous people and must compete with them if he is to survive. To put it in modern terms, he must learn to swim with the sharks. Therefore, the prince must know how to behave badly and to use this knowledge as a tool to maintain his power. Machiavelli recognizes that princes are always in the public eye. Their behavior will affect their public image, and their reputation will affect their ability to keep power. With this in mind, Machiavelli advises that it is fine to avoid vices, but because no one can avoid them all, the prince should be careful to avoid those that will most severely damage his reputation and, therefore, his power. His consciousness of a prince's need to control his public image would not seem out of place in the media age, where public relations experts carefully groom and prepare politicians for public consumption. Apparently flaunting all conventional moral advice, he says that many things that appear good will damage a prince's power, while those that appear bad will enhance it.

The contrast between the imaginary world of virtues and the real world of vices could not be more plain. Now that he has everyone's attention, he proceeds to dissect these so-called virtues in the next three chapters.

Glossary

Tuscan the variety of Italian spoken in Tuscany, the region of Italy where Florence is located.

Chapter 16

Summary

A reputation for generosity is thought to be desirable, but developing it can be dangerous. Generosity exercised in truly virtuous ways is never seen by others, so if you want to be thought of as a generous ruler, you must keep up a lavish public display. To support this habit, a prince must raise taxes and squeeze money from his subjects. Generosity of this sort benefits few and harms many. The prince's subjects will hate him, and no one will respect him because he is poor. Therefore, a wise prince will not mind being called a miser, because stinginess is a vice that allows him to reign. If a prince is giving away other people's property, he can afford to be generous, but if he is giving away his own resources, he will become grasping and hated or poor and despised.

Commentary

After teasing the reader with shocking revelations in Chapter 15, Machiavelli comes away sounding thoroughly conservative in this chapter, discussing the supposed virtue of generosity. His focus is on the appearance of generosity and what one must do to develop one's public image. True generosity, he notes, would not get a prince a reputation for being generous, because no one would see it. This is an important distinction. Machiavelli does not say that true generosity is bad. What concerns him is the kind of forced display that a prince must put on to develop a public image as a generous man. Supporting lavish displays eventually makes a prince poor, forcing him to exploit his subjects' resources. This does real harm to everyone, including the prince. Thus the supposed virtue is no virtue at all.

He does qualify this observation by saying that new princes who are trying to gain power must be seen to be generous, but after they have power, they should immediately curtail their spending. He offers good examples: Both Louis XII of France and Ferdinand of Spain were noted for their thrifty habits, and both were energetic conquerors. On the subject of conquerors, Machiavelli makes the interesting observation that because armies live off looting and extortion, a leader of armies had better be generous or his soldiers may decide to leave. According to Machiavelli, this is desirable, because the property involved is not the prince's or his subjects', and therefore the integrity of the state is not harmed.

Glossary

Caesar Julius Caesar had a reputation for generosity that contributed to his popularity. He was assassinated in 44 B.C., only a year after his triumphal return to Rome from a series of military victories.

Chapter 17

Summary

Every prince will want to be considered merciful, but mercy should not be mismanaged. Cesare Borgia, by being cruel, restored peace and order to the Romagna. No prince should mind being called cruel for keeping his subjects peaceful and loyal. Punishing a few, and thus averting disorder, is better than allowing troubles to develop that will hurt many. New rulers cannot avoid seeming cruel, because their states are insecure. Still, a prince should not be too rash or too fearful.

If you cannot be both loved and feared, then it is better to be feared than loved. Men are generally fickle, afraid of danger, and greedy. When a prince benefits them, they will do anything for the prince, but when trouble comes, they will desert the prince. People will break ties of love if it is to their advantage, but fear of punishment they will never transgress. A prince must be careful not to make himself hated, even though he is feared; to do this, he must keep his hands off his subjects' property and their women. People will sooner forget the death of a father than the loss of an inheritance. However, when a prince commands an army, he must be cruel in order to control his troops.

Theme

In conclusion, people love at their own wish, but fear at the prince's will, so a wise ruler will rely on what he can best control.

Commentary

Continuing his discussion of virtues that are not virtues, Machiavelli considers mercy and cruelty. As with generosity and miserliness, he comes down on the side of the supposedly bad quality. He bases his judgment on consideration of what benefits the most people. It is no use to be merciful if by doing so, a prince allows disorder in his state to get out of control. A controlled amount of cruelty, which harms a few, can avert widespread violence and lawlessness, which harms many. Mercy that allows the majority to suffer cannot properly be called mercy. This is an extremely old idea in Western jurisprudence, and one can still hear it cited as a justification for the imposition of punishment for crimes: Failing to punish wrongdoers penalizes the innocent people who would be harmed by the criminal's future actions. As an example, Machiavelli praises Cesare Borgia's policy of subduing the lawless Romagna region, described in Chapter 8. He also criticizes the Florentine government for failing to intervene when civil war broke out in Pistoia, a Florentine possession. Though the Florentines sent Machiavelli to investigate the situation, they did nothing, and as a result, many citizens died in the fighting.

Machiavelli is careful not to advocate cruelty for cruelty's sake. As in Chapter 8, he warns the prince not to constantly injure his subjects, because this will make him hated. Instead, he must be cruel only when necessary to avoid greater wrongs. Even his assertion that the leaders of armies must be cruel is based on the maintenance of discipline, for undisciplined armies harm innocent citizens—or even the ruler himself. This philosophy leads him to the logical conclusion that if a prince has to choose between being loved and being feared, being feared is at least safer, for both the ruler and his subjects.

Character Insight

Machiavelli's typically dark view of human nature is on display in this chapter, as seen in his warning about those who swear they love you in good times, but then desert you in bad times. The most cynical of Machiavelli's statements in this chapter is his assertion that people are quicker to forgive the death of a loved one than the confiscation of their property—there could be no bleaker assessment of raw human selfishness. Surrounded by people like these, a prince is indeed safer if he can control them by fear, because love is so fleeting and unreliable.

Glossary

Dido founder and queen of Carthage: In the *Aeneid* she falls in love with Aeneas and kills herself when he leaves her.

Hannibal (247–183 B.C.) Carthaginian general: crossed the Alps to invade Italy in 218. He was defeated by Scipio Africanus in 202 B.C. Fabius Maximus, more conservative in his tactics than Scipio, also fought against Hannibal.

Locri a city captured by Scipio and brutally treated by one of his commanders.

Chapter 18

Summary

Everyone knows that princes should keep their word, but we see that the princes who have accomplished the most have been accomplished at deception. A prince may fight with laws, which is the way of human beings, or with force, which is the way of animals. A prince should imitate the fox in cunning as well as the lion in strength. A wise prince should never keep his word when it would go against his interest, because he can expect others to do the same. In order to pull it off, you must be a good liar, but you will always find people willing to be deceived.

Theme

To sum it up, it is useful to seem to be virtuous, but you must be ready to act the opposite way if the situation requires it. A prince should do good if he can, but be ready to do evil if he must. Yet a prince must be careful to always act in a way that appears virtuous, for many can see you, but few know how you really are. If a ruler conquers and maintains his state, everyone will praise him, judging his actions by their outcome.

Commentary

This chapter concludes Machiavelli's discussion of the qualities a prince should display. Keeping his feet firmly in the real world, as he promised, he begins by stating that even though everyone assumes princes should keep their word, experience shows that those who do not keep their word get the better of those who do. This is Machiavelli's justification for deceit: Because you can expect other princes not to honor their word to you, you should not feel obligated to honor your word to them. Sebastian de Grazia, writing about this chapter, refers to Machiavelli's precept as the "Un-Golden Rule"—do unto others as you can expect they will do unto you. In this bestial world, princes must act like beasts, imitating the clever fox, instead of relying only on strength, as does the lion. In a world full of deceivers, there must also be someone to deceive, and Machiavelli finds that there are plenty of people willing to overlook all kinds of deceit as long as their state is peaceful and prosperous.

Theme

The prince's control of his public image gets special attention in this chapter. A prince must always appear to be truthful, merciful, and religious, even if he must sometimes act in the opposite way. Interestingly, these are the very same qualities he condemns Agathocles for lacking in Chapter 8, but here, he advises the prince to dispense with them when necessary. But the great mass of people will never see the prince as he really is; they will see only the image he projects. The few insiders who know the prince's true nature will do nothing to harm him as long as the people support him, and the people will support him as long as he has been successful. Here, Machiavelli sounds remarkably like a modern spin doctor advising a politician on how to get good press.

Glossary

Chiron the wisest of all centaurs (half-man and half-horse), famous for his knowledge of medicine: he is the teacher of Asclepius, Achilles, and Hercules.

prince who is not named the reference is to King Ferdinand of Spain, who had a wide reputation for being deceptive and crafty.

Chapter 19

Summary

A prince must avoid becoming hated or despised. Taking the property or the women of his subjects will make him hated. Being frivolous, indecisive, and effeminate will make him despised. All a prince's actions should show seriousness, strength, and decisiveness. The best defense against internal threats such as conspiracy is to be neither hated nor despised. If a conspirator thinks that killing the prince will enrage the people, he will think twice.

Wise princes are careful not to antagonize the nobles and to keep the people happy. In France, the parliament restrains the ambition of the nobles and favors the people, without directly involving the king, so that he cannot be accused of favoritism. Princes should let others do the unpleasant tasks, doing for themselves what will make them look good.

Some people may object that the careers of the Roman emperors go against this argument, because many of them were greatly admired, yet were still assassinated. This is because they had to deal with their soldiers, and they could not satisfy both the soldiers, who wanted warlike leaders, and the people, who wanted peace. Marcus, Pertinax, and Alexander were all compassionate and just, but only Marcus escaped assassination, because he was a hereditary ruler and did not owe his power to the army. Commodus, Severus, Antoninus, and Maximinus were all cruel and greedy, and only Severus escaped assassination, because he was so cunning and ruthless, and because he kept up a splendid reputation. But in Machiavelli's time, princes do not have the same need to satisfy their armies, because armies are not used to being together for long periods and controlling whole provinces, the way Roman armies were. Instead, princes should satisfy the people, who are more powerful.

Commentary

Conspiracy and assassination occupy Machiavelli's attention in this chapter. The best way to avoid these dangers is to avoid being hated or despised by one's subjects. (By *despised*, Machiavelli means to be held in contempt or to be regarded with no respect.) In the state, there are two main groups the prince must court: the nobles and the people, a theme pulled from Chapter 9. Although a prince must not alienate the nobles, he must win over the people, because they are the majority, and their ill will can cost a prince his place and his life. Hated and despised princes are targets for assassination, because assassins conclude that the people will support killing the ruler.

Plots such as these were a real concern for Renaissance rulers. Machiavelli offers as an example the 1445 assassination of Annibale Bentivoglio, ruler of Bologna, noting that popular support enabled the family to keep their power despite their desperate situation after the assassination. In Machiavelli's own lifetime, in Florence in 1478, the Pazzi conspiracy against the Medici had resulted in the injury of Lorenzo the Magnificent and the death of Lorenzo's brother. In both cases the assassins were from rival powerful families; they were not disgruntled subjects. As if acknowledging this, Machiavelli observes that there is no real defense against a determined assassin, because anyone who is not afraid to die can kill a ruler. Nonetheless, he maintains that popular support is the best prevention.

About balancing the conflicting demands of the people and the nobles, Machiavelli offers the interesting example of France's parliamentary government, which allowed participation by both the aristocracy and the commoners. Rather than presenting it as a democratic innovation, he offers it as a way of increasing the absolute ruler's power, taking pressure off of the prince by putting competing interests into a neutral forum—in effect, giving unpleasant tasks to others so they do not damage the prince's popularity.

Theme

In the midst of his argument, Machiavelli embarks on a long digression about the many Roman emperors, good and bad, who were assassinated. He concludes that most of them were undone by their powerful and bloodthirsty armies, a problem that the princes of Machiavelli's time need not worry about. His more interesting observation, which is somewhat lost in his analysis, is that nearly all of the rulers were killed regardless of their qualities and actions. Some did one thing and others did the opposite, but all came to basically the same end. The key to their success or failure is whether they adapted their actions to their times and political circumstances. This theme reappears in Chapter 25, where Machiavelli discusses the effect of fortune on human affairs.

Glossary

Marcus Marcus Aurelius (161–180), called "the Philosopher;" one of the most respected of the Roman emperors.

Commodus (161–192), oldest son of Marcus Aurelius. Noted as an enthusiast for gladiator and wild animal games in the Coliseum. Assassinated by a group of conspirators.

Pertinax (126–193). After Commodus was assassinated, Pertinax was proclaimed emperor by the praetorian guard, but was assassinated three months later by rebellious soldiers.

Julianus (died 193) After the assassination of Pertinax, Julianus bought the office of emperor from the praetorian guard, but was assassinated by order of the Senate two months later.

Severus Septimius Severus (145–211). Proclaimed emperor by the Senate. Overcame claims to the throne by Pescennius Niger and Clodius Albinus. He died while on a military campaign in England.

Antoninus Caracalla Marcus Aurelius Antoninus (188–217), called Caracalla. Oldest son of Septimius Severus. He was killed by the prefect of the praetorian guard, Macrinus.

Macrinus Marcus Opellius Severus (circa 164–218) spent all of his brief reign on military campaigns in Asia. He was executed by his opponents.

Heliogabalus also called Elagabalus (circa 204–225), Heliogabalus was killed by the praetorian guard.

Alexander Marcus Aurelius Severus Alexander (208–235). Succeeded his cousin Heliogabalus. Killed by rebellious soldiers in Gaul.

Maximinus (died 238) named emperor by the army after Alexander Severus was killed. Subsequently killed by his own troops.

Chapter 20

Summary

Princes have tried various tactics to maintain power: disarming their subjects, dividing their subjects into factions, encouraging their enemies, winning over the suspicious, building new fortresses, and tearing down fortresses.

New princes must never disarm their subjects, for if a prince arms his people, their arms become his. If a prince disarms them, the people will hate him, and he will be forced to employ mercenaries.

Conventional wisdom says that creating factions is a good way to control a state. This may have been true when Italy was more stable, but not in Machiavelli's time. When factious cities are threatened by invaders, they quickly fall.

Because rulers become great by overcoming difficulties, some believe that a prince should secretly encourage his enemies, so that when he overcomes them, his reputation will be greater.

Some new princes find that those who were at first suspect prove more useful than others in governing the state. They are anxious to prove themselves to the prince. Those who helped the prince gain power may have done so out of dissatisfaction with the prior state, and the new state may also fail to please them.

Princes often build fortresses to protect themselves from plotters and sudden attacks. If a prince fears his subjects more than foreign invaders, he should build fortresses. The best fortress, however, is not to be hated by the people.

Commentary

In this chapter, Machiavelli briefly discusses a number of potential strategies for maintaining power. Predictably, he opposes disarming one's subjects, having already expressed his support for citizen armies over mercenaries or outside troops. Disarming citizens also sends a message that the prince does not trust them, and Machiavelli highly values a good relationship between the prince and his subjects. Like disarming one's subjects, building fortresses within the city also expresses distrust and shows insecurity. No fortress can substitute for the trust and support of the people.

Encouraging rival factions to fight in order to keep them occupied also is the mark of a weak and insecure ruler. Machiavelli alludes to the Florentine policy in Pistoia, which he already condemned as cruel in Chapter 17. He blamed factionalism for some of Italy's problems, pointing out that divided cities fall easily when foreign invaders come, because one side or the other sells out to the invaders in hopes of gaining power. Oddly, Machiavelli expresses no opinion about the practice of secretly encouraging one's enemies in order to gain glory by overcoming them later, merely mentioning it without discussing it.

Machiavelli devotes the largest portion of this chapter to making the point that those people who are under suspicion turn out to be the most trustworthy servants of the new prince. This should be no surprise, considering that Machiavelli was distrusted by the new Medici leadership, to whom he dedicated *The Prince* in the hope of regaining his old position as a diplomat. It is easy to imagine Machiavelli speaking about himself when he points out that those who are insecure in their positions work harder and are more motivated to prove themselves to the prince than those whom the prince trusts. He observes that those who were unhappy under the previous regime (unlike Machiavelli) may be just as likely to become unhappy with the new prince, while those who most love the stability of the state (like Machiavelli) will necessarily prove more loyal.

Glossary

Guelphs supporters of Papal interests. Their opponents, the Ghibellines, were supporters of the Holy Roman Empire.

Pandolfo Petrucci (1450–1512) ruler of Siena. It is not clear to what "suspected men" Machiavelli is referring.

Niccolò Vitelli (1414–1486) mercenary leader, father of Paolo and Vitellozo Vitelli. He became leader of Città de Castello and destroyed several fortresses built there by his opponent, Pope Sixtus IV.

Countess of Forli Caterina Sforza Riario (1463–1509). Her husband was Girolamo Riario (1443–1488). Negotiations with Caterina were the subject of Machiavelli's very first diplomatic assignment in July 1499. When her husband was assassinated, she held out against the revolt in one of her fortresses until help arrived from her uncle, Ludovico Sforza of Milan. When Cesare Borgia invaded in late 1499, her subjects welcomed him and again revolted against her, and she was forced to surrender despite the protection of her fortress.

Chapter 21

Summary

Nothing enhances a ruler's reputation more than undertaking great conquests. Ferdinand of Spain's career provides a good example. He had attacked Granada; driven the Moors out of Spain; and attacked Africa, Italy, and France. These activities kept his subjects amazed and preoccupied, so that no one had time to do anything against him.

With regard to internal affairs, princes should always find noteworthy ways to reward or punish any extraordinary actions.

Rulers must never remain neutral. If neighboring rulers fight, you must take sides, because if you do not, the winner will threaten you, and the loser will not befriend you. Whether or not your ally wins, he will be grateful to you. However, if you can avoid it, you should never ally with someone more powerful than yourself, because if he wins, you may be in his power.

A prince should show that he loves talent and rewards it. He should encourage his citizens to prosper in their occupations. He should keep the people entertained with festivals at appropriate times. And he should give attention to the various civic groups, attending some of their activities, but without appearing undignified.

Commentary

Theme

Reputation and public image are the topics of this chapter. Conquests and daring deeds are the first way to enhance one's reputation. King Ferdinand of Spain is Machiavelli's exemplar, but he gets ambiguous treatment. Although Machiavelli calls him the most famous and glorious prince in Christendom, he also has harsh words for Ferdinand's expulsion of the Moors from Spain, calling it a despicable act done under a religious pretext. In Chapter 18, Machiavelli made a not-very-subtle reference to Ferdinand's penchant for trickery and deceit. Clearly he admires Ferdinand's boldness and energy, but deplores his actions. The emphasis on Ferdinand's ability to keep his subjects amazed and preoccupied recalls the description of Cesare Borgia's execution of Remirro de Orco, which left the people stunned and satisfied. Machiavelli specifically mentions public spectacles at the end of this chapter, and there is a suggestion that spectacle, whether in the form of entertaining festivals, dramatic executions, or daring schemes, is one of the prince's most important tools for controlling public opinion. In the same way, rewarding citizens' achievements or punishing their misdeeds should have an element of spectacle. It should make people talk, and when they talk, it should be about how remarkable the prince is.

Machiavelli's other recommendation has to do with decisiveness. Not surprisingly, given his preference for bold action, Machiavelli deplores princes who try to remain neutral in disputes. He presents this as a practical consideration: If a prince fails to take sides, he may find himself without friends when the dust settles. In this discussion, Machiavelli makes one of his few positive statements about human behavior, remarking that men are not so dishonorable nor ungrateful that they will immediately turn on their allies. Given Machiavelli's own advice to the prince in Chapter 18 to break his word when it suits his goals, the reader may have difficulty taking seriously Machiavelli's assurances in this case.

Returning to his theme of maintaining good relationships with one's subjects, Machiavelli says that a prince should reward merit and encourage prosperity, because achievements by the citizens improve the state. Princes should show themselves to be friendly to their subjects but without compromising the dignity of their office. Maintaining a certain distance keeps an air of grandeur intact.

Glossary

Moors Islamic residents of Spain, the Moors had invaded from north Africa in the early eighth century and controlled large portions of Spain until Ferdinand drove them out during the Reconquest, completed by 1500. Ferdinand expelled the Jews at the same time, in his desire to make Spain a pure Christian nation. Machiavelli implies that this was a purely political maneuver done under a religious pretext.

Bernabò Bernabò Visconti (1323–1385), ruler of Milan, was famous for giving bizarre punishments.

Chapters 22 and 23

Summary

Choosing good ministers is vital, because a ruler shows his intelligence in his choice of the men around him. If a man cannot have good ideas himself, he must be smart enough to distinguish his minister's good ideas from his bad ones. The minister must think always of the prince, not of himself. The prince should honor and reward his minister, so that the minister will be dependent on the prince.

Unless rulers are shrewd about choosing their advisors, they will find themselves surrounded by flatterers. The only way to guard against flattery is to show that you are not offended by the truth. But if anyone can speak their mind to you, you will not be respected. A wise prince will pick intelligent advisors and allow only them to speak frankly, and only when he asks for their opinions. He should listen carefully, but make his own decisions and stick to them.

A prince who is not wise can never get good counsel, unless he puts himself completely in the hands of a wise man; but such a man will soon take over his state. An ignorant prince who takes advice from several counselors will never be able to reconcile their conflicting opinions, for each minister will think of his own interests. Men will always be disloyal unless a prince forces them to be faithful.

Commentary

These two brief chapters deal with the advisors and ministers whom a prince chooses to aid him. Machiavelli's discussion of the topic is direct and yet contradictory. A prudent ruler, even if he is not unusually intelligent, may choose a brilliant advisor, and so be thought wise. Then again, a ruler who is not wise can never get good advice, because he cannot evaluate it properly. A good minister will be dedicated to the state and think of nothing but the prince's interests; but ministers will always forward their own interests unless a prince compels them to be loyal to him. Machiavelli's typically dark view of human nature runs up against his view that good ministers are indispensable to a prince. Because

Machiavelli himself had been a "good minister" in the Florentine republic and genuinely hoped to get that position back, it is not surprising that he emphasizes the value of a minister who is truly devoted to the affairs of state.

As in Chapter 21, Machiavelli states that a prince should display decisiveness, directness, and dignity. Princes must value—and even insist on—complete candor from their advisors. Then again, if they allow too much freedom of opinion, they compromise their dignity by making themselves too approachable. The warning against flatterers was a standard caution in Renaissance advice books.

Glossary

Antonio da Venafro Antonio Giordani was a lawyer employed as a minister by Pandolfo Petrucci, ruler of Siena.

Maximilian Emperor Maximilian I (1459–1519), ruler of the Holy Roman Empire. Father Luca Raimondi was one of his advisors. Machiavelli had an opportunity to observe Maximillian when Machiavelli visited Maximillian's court on a diplomatic mission from 1507 to 1508.

Chapter 24

Summary

If a new prince follows all of these principles, he will soon be as secure as a hereditary ruler, because if people find they are doing well in the present, they will not look for changes. But anyone who acquires a new state and then loses it through incompetence is disgraced. The Italian rulers who have lost their states did so because they lacked military power, made their subjects hate them, or were unable to defend against the nobles. They should not blame bad luck but their own laziness for their losses, because they did not make preparations, and when trouble struck, they ran away, hoping the people would restore them. A prince can only rely on defenses that he can personally control.

Commentary

This chapter brings Machiavelli back to his discussion of Italy's political situation in his time, which he last treated in his discussion of military matters in Chapters 12 through 14. He specifically mentions the King of Naples and the Duke of Milan as rulers who have lost their power, but he is most concerned with Ludovico Sforza, whom Machiavelli regarded with contempt. Sforza provided a perfect example of how not to follow Machiavelli's precepts. He encouraged Charles VIII of France to invade Italy, and when Louis XII returned, the French deprived Sforza of his state and made him their prisoner. Machiavelli blamed him for many of Italy's troubles resulting from the foreign invasions. Frederick of Aragon (1452–1504), the King of Naples, is probably less fair as an example, because he was forced out of power by a secret agreement between Louis XII and Ferdinand II to divide Naples between them. In the face of two major powers, there was very little Frederick could have done to preserve his position.

Theme

In particular, Machiavelli has harsh words for the laziness and indolence of the Italian princes, because an ideal prince must always be planning and maneuvering to avoid future disasters. Finally, Machiavelli returns to his theme of self-sufficiency: Relying on others is always a mistake, because others are out of your control. Only by controlling your own resources can you be really secure. Machiavelli takes up this theme more fully in Chapter 25.

Glossary

Philip of Macedon Philip V (238–179 B.C.), king of Macedon. He was defeated in 197 B.C. by Titus Quintus Flaminius, a Roman general, at Cynoscephalae.

Chapter 25

Summary

Many people believe that fortune controls everything, so that there is no use in trying to act, but fortune controls only half of one's actions, leaving free will to control the other half. Fortune can be compared to a river that floods, destroying everything in its way. But when the weather is good, people can prepare dams and dikes to control the flood. If Italy had such preparations, she would not have suffered so much in the present floods.

Princes are successful one day and ruined the next, with no change in their natures. Two men may use the same method, but only one succeeds; and two men may use different methods, but reach the same goal, all because the circumstances do or do not suit their actions. If a man is successful by acting one way and the circumstances change, he will fail if he does not change his methods. But men are never flexible enough to change, either because their natures will not let them or because they become accustomed to a certain behavior bringing success.

It is better to be bold than timid and cautious, because fortune is a woman, and the man who wants to control her must treat her roughly.

Commentary

This chapter is perhaps the most pivotal in *The Prince*, because Machiavelli discusses the relationship of action and fortune in determining the prince's success. Machiavelli uses *fortune* (*fortuna*) in at least two senses. In Chapters 7 and 8, Machiavelli contrasts *virtù* with fortune in the sense of luck or the favor of powerful people. In those chapters, the contrast is between what the prince can control (his own actions) and what he cannot control (the favor of others). In this chapter, fortune refers more to prevailing circumstances and events, which are still things that the prince cannot directly control. Rather than taking the fatalistic view that all events are controlled by destiny and that it is useless to work toward a particular outcome, Machiavelli gives fortune control over only half of human actions, letting free will influence the rest. If free will did not operate, all of a prince's *virtù* would be for nothing.

Yet Machiavelli struggles with the problem of why one person succeeds and another fails, even though they have employed the same methods, or why totally different methods can arrive at the same outcome. To explain this, he proposes that success comes when *virtù* is suited to the particular situation a prince finds himself in. Machiavelli envisions fortune as a set of constantly changing circumstances in which particular actions can bring about success or failure. To describe it, he uses one of his few extended metaphors, making fortune a force of nature, like a river that seems uncontrollable, yet can be tamed and directed by human activity. If the Italian princes had made suitable preparations, the "flood" of foreign invasions would not have swept over the open and unprotected country.

Having affirmed the value of free will, Machiavelli limits it by asserting that even though it may be possible to vary one's actions to suit the times, no one ever does. Machiavelli implies that this is because *virtù* is an inherent, natural quality that the prince cannot change. People act according to their character and cannot change their natures. This line of reasoning brings Machiavelli back to the pessimistic fatalism he rejected at the beginning of the chapter. If a prince cannot change his nature, success depends simply on being lucky enough to have a character suited to the times he lives in.

Fortune was frequently personified in Renaissance art and literature as *Fortuna*, a female figure who held a turning wheel to symbolize her constant state of change. Fortuna's fickleness is her greatest trait; no sooner are you at the top of her wheel than it turns, and you end up at the bottom. Drawing on this symbolism, Machiavelli closes the chapter by saying that a man who wants to subdue fortune must treat her like the woman she is, and approach her with boldness and roughness. While Machiavelli's metaphor may be offensive to some modern readers, it would not have been shocking in its own day. Even in modern times, the saying "fortune favors the bold" can still be heard.

Glossary

Julius the warlike pope's remarkable career as a military leader was cut short by his sudden death in 1513.

Chapter 26

Summary

There could not be a more appropriate time to welcome a new ruler to Italy. In order for the greatness of Italian spirit to be shown, Italy had to be humiliated first. Although it appeared a prince was coming to lead her, bad luck struck him down, so that she still waits eagerly for her rescuer.

The Medici family can fill this role, if they will imitate the precepts Machiavelli has explained. Even signs from God point to their coming greatness. The other Italian princes never achieved this goal, because their old methods of warfare were unsound. There is no lack of courage or strength among the Italians, but their leaders are weak. For this reason, Italian armies have lost in the field for the last 20 years. If the Medici family want to become great leaders, they will raise their own armies. All the other European armies, despite their successes, have weaknesses that can be exploited with new strategies.

Italy has been waiting for a savior to liberate her from oppression by the foreign barbarians. Let the Medici take up the cause, and Italy will be great once more.

Commentary

Style & Language

The final chapter of *The Prince* is Machiavelli's exhortation to the Medici family to lead Italy out of foreign domination under a strong, centralized leadership. His tone is passionate and poetic, in contrast to the dry, direct style of the rest of the book. Still, Machiavelli slips back into his more familiar analytical style when discussing the various military techniques employed by the German, Swiss, French, and Spanish. Methods of warfare were another of Machiavelli's great interests. In 1520, he wrote an entire book on the subject in his *Art of War* (*Dell'Arte della guerra*). Machiavelli is at his most fervent when describing the bravery and strength of the Italian national spirit, and he rebukes the foolish leaders who have failed to make use of this great raw material. Even here, though, he has room for a small jab: The Italians, he says, fight well individually, but do not take well to authority, because they all think they know best.

Another notable break with the rest of the book is the repeated invocation of God, who has been conspicuously absent from Machiavelli's discussion up until this point: Italy beseeches God for a redeemer, God favors the Medici, God wants the people to use free will, and God sends signs to show that the time is near. Machiavelli even refers to the man who was thought to have been ordained by God to save Italy, namely Cesare Borgia, who but for his rotten luck would have unified Italy. Italy still waits for this promised savior.

The bitterness of Italy's subjugation to foreign powers runs throughout this final chapter. All of Machiavelli's observations and advice about the state and the prince have been directed toward this goal, to bring forth the leader who will liberate Italy from the barbarians and unify it. Then Italy will be the peaceful, prosperous state Machiavelli envisions, with a prince who works for the security and stability his subjects need. Machiavelli closes the book with a quotation from the patriotic poem "My Italy" (*Italia mia*) by the great Italian poet Francesco Petrarca.

Glossary

Moses, Cyrus, Theseus the great leaders Machiavelli cited in Chapter 6, whom he presents here as liberators of oppressed peoples.

head of the Church Giovanni de Medici, the newly elected Pope Leo X.

Sea, cloud, stone, manna miracles that occurred when Moses led the Israelites out of slavery in Egypt. Machiavelli claims these are signs that point to the Medici's role in liberating Italy.

Taro . . . Mestre battles in which Italian forces were defeated.

CHARACTER ANALYSES

The Medici Family

The Medici family were the most powerful citizens of Florence, leaders of the largest bank in Europe, and through strategic marriage alliances, joined many of Europe's royal families.

The founder of the family fortunes was Giovanni di Bicci de Medici (1360–1429). Under his leadership, the family bank blossomed, and he soon became the richest man in Florence. Banking was a relative innovation during the period, and the Medici were its most successful practitioners. Giovanni's son, Cosimo (1389–1464), called Cosimo the Elder, succeeded him as leader of the bank. Though nominally an ordinary Florentine citizen, Cosimo skillfully manipulated Florence's political institutions to his family's benefit, using his wealth and connections to pack the governmental bodies with Medici supporters, until he was all but official ruler of Florence.

His son Piero (1416–1469) briefly succeeded him, but it was Piero's son Lorenzo (1449–1492), called Lorenzo the Magnificent, who presided over the Medici golden age and, by extension, the golden age of Florence. He earned his nickname by spending lavishly on artistic and architectural projects to beautify Florence and on splendid public festivals to entertain its citizens. Like his father and grandfather, he maintained control of Florence by making sure that his supporters were appointed to key positions in the government, so that he remained technically an ordinary citizen while living like a prince. In 1478, he survived an assassination attempt by the Pazzi, a rival banking family supported by his enemy, Pope Sixtus IV. He was attacked as he attended church services at the cathedral of Florence. His brother Giovanni was killed, but Lorenzo suffered only minor wounds. The conspirators were hunted down and vengefully executed; the noted artist Sandro Boticelli commemorated the executions in a series of murals. A war with Sixtus followed, in which Lorenzo turned for help to the French and finally ended the war with a dramatic personal visit to the Pope's chief ally, Ferrante of Naples. Subsequently, Lorenzo's position was completely secure, and he became an important stabilizing influence on the Italian states, maintaining a network of formal alliances and friendly personal relationships which helped to keep the peace on the Italian peninsula. Unfortunately, he also neglected management of the family bank, which suffered huge losses near the end of his lifetime. Lorenzo's lavish spending and competition from younger rival banks sapped the family fortune, but the family's influence and reputation remained.

Lorenzo's son Piero (1472–1503) succeeded him as acknowledged ruler of Florence, but proved as unpopular as his father had been popular. When Charles VIII of France invaded Italy in 1494, Piero initially denied him passage through Florentine territory. But as Charles' army approached the city, Piero panicked. He went to the French camp and surrendered Florence to Charles without a struggle. Already disenchanted with Piero and outraged by his concessions to the French, the Florentines rebelled. A democratic faction led by Friar Girolamo Savonarola drove the Medici out of the city and declared it a republic. The Medici would not return until the fall of the next republic, in which Machiavelli served as secretary, in 1512.

The Medici rose to power through their immense wealth and their skill in arranging alliances rather than through military conquest, making them unique among Italian princes of their time. In particular, they systematically married into almost all the great royal families of Europe. Lorenzo the Magnificent's granddaughter Catherine de Medici (1519–1589) became queen mother of France. The Medici also produced two popes, Leo X and Clement VII, who focused their attention on promoting the family's power and influence.

Savonarola

The republic that succeeded the Medici in 1492 was a peculiar political institution, having apocalyptic religious fervor as its driving force. Its leader was Girolamo Savonarola (1452–1498), a friar of the Dominican order who had come to Florence as a preacher in 1481. His personality was so charismatic and his sermons so vivid and emotionally stirring that he soon had his audiences spellbound. He drew a varied group of disciples, including artists and members of noble families. Savonarola was a reformer who railed against the luxurious extravagances of the Florentines and the sins of Italy in general. He also claimed to be a prophet, having predicted the deaths of several rulers and a coming time of retribution when Italy would be conquered. When Charles VIII invaded, Savonarola declared it the punishment of God for the sins of the Italian people.

When Piero de Medici was deposed, Savonarola and his followers set up a kind of theocracy in place of the Medici government. To his credit, he reformed the institutions that the Medici had turned into props for their own power. But policy was directed by the will of God as Savonarola interpreted it, and disagreement with such policies was a sin. In an excess of reforming zeal, he commanded the Florentines to give up all vices and luxuries that tempted them to sin, and many of them happily did so. In 1497, an immense pile of artwork, literature, gambling equipment, fashionable clothing, carnival masks, jewelry, and other sinful frivolities was burned in a public square, an event known as "the Bonfire of the Vanities." Savonarola, preaching almost daily, vowed to make Florence the New Jerusalem, the city of God on earth, and foretold that when this was accomplished, the new age of universal peace would begin.

Chief among the sinners that Savonarola denounced was the infamous Pope Alexander VI, whose riches and lascivious lifestyle perfectly represented the corruption that Savonarola sought to purge. Savonarola's opponents in Florence, urged on by Alexander, were becoming more vocal, and bad economic times in Florence meant that Savanarola's influence was waning. Gangs of young aristocrats harassed Savonarola's followers and heckled him during his sermons. The Franciscan order, traditional rivals of Savonarola's Dominicans, demanded that he show some evidence of his holiness and proposed a trial by fire. Representatives from both orders met in the piazza on April 7, 1498, but the contest was delayed by squabbles over what items the contestants could carry into the fire with them, and a rainstorm finally led to the cancellation of the event. It was perceived that the entire event had been a sham from the start, and Savonarola's charismatic hold over the populace was broken. The next day, a mob attacked his church, and he was put in prison. He and two fellow friars were hanged in May 1498, their bodies burned, and their ashes thrown in the Arno river. In June, Machiavelli would take up his post in the new republican government.

The Borgia Family

The Borgia family originated in Spain, where the family name was spelled "Borja." When Cardinal Alfonso de Borja was unexpectedly elected Pope Calixtus III in 1455, the career of the Borgias was launched. In 1456, Calixtus made his nephew Rodrigo, then only 25 years old, a cardinal and vice-chancellor of the church. Rodrigo used his position to acquire lucrative church offices and build alliances that would eventually allow him to maneuver his own election as Pope Alexander VI in 1492. Expert at accumulating wealth both for himself and the church, Alexander would use his money to maintain a luxurious court and to advance the position of his family.

Sensuous by nature and notoriously attractive to women, Alexander openly kept a series of mistresses, most notably Vannozza Catenei, a Roman beauty who bore him four children. In all, he had nine children, including two born after he became pope. Alexander shamelessly used his children as political pawns, plotting strategic marriages to establish a Borgia dynasty. He arranged three marriages for his unfortunate daughter Lucrezia: When her first husband, a member of the Sforza family, proved no longer politically useful, Alexander annulled the marriage, publicly claiming that the groom was impotent. Alexander then married Lucrezia to a prince of Naples, who was murdered a few years later by a gang of thugs, supposedly because Borgia policy toward Naples had changed. She was then married to Alfonso d'Este of Ferrara, who agreed only after a combination of threats and bribes from Alexander. Happily for Lucrezia, she became loved and respected as the lady of Ferrara.

Alexander's most famous child was Cesare, his second son. Originally marked for a career in the church, Cesare became a cardinal in 1493 at the scandalously young age of 18. In 1497, his older brother Juan, his father's favorite, disappeared. His body, bearing nine stab wounds, was found floating in the Tiber river a few days later. Cesare was rumored to have arranged the murder. Whether or not he was responsible, the murder completely changed Cesare's situation. The next year, he renounced his cardinalate and went to France to give the new king, Louis XII, the marriage annulment he had requested from Alexander, getting in exchange a French princess for a bride and the help of the French armies to conquer the Romagna. This region was traditionally a part of the Papal States, but was not under firm control. In 1499, he began his conquests, and by 1501, he had been named Duke of Romagna by his father. In 1502, he conquered Urbino and Camerino, and a group of his allies, feeling threatened by his success, formed a conspiracy against him. They were unsuccessful, and Cesare, pretending forgiveness, invited them to a meeting at Senigallia, where he had all of them executed.

Cesare was at the height of his power in 1503 when Alexander suddenly died. Without his father's political influence and money, Cesare's resources dried up. Hated and feared by many in Rome for his ruthless tactics and his lust for power, he found himself without friends. The election of a sworn Borgia enemy, Giuliano della Rovere, as Pope Julius II, sealed Cesare's fate. Ferdinand of Spain, an ally of the new pope, had Cesare arrested and imprisoned in 1504, but in 1506 Cesare escaped to France, where he worked as a captain for his brother-in-law, the King of Navarre. He was killed in a minor battle in 1507.

The Borgia reputation for cunning, decadence, sensuality, and brutality was firmly based in reality, but malicious gossip and the popular imagination exaggerated it to fantastic proportions. For centuries, historians portrayed the Borgias as the grand villains of the Italian Renaissance. Cesare was believed to have murdered not only his brother and his rebellious captains, but also his sister's second husband and numerous others who either offended him or stood in his way. The Borgias were also believed to have been expert poisoners, and almost every unexplained death among their opponents was attributed to poison. Machiavelli's unqualified admiration for Cesare's methods reinforced both their reputations as diabolical figures.

The Sforza Family

The founder of the Sforza dynasty was Muzio Attendolo Sforza (1369–1424). The son of a peasant family, he became a successful *condottiere*, a professional soldier for hire. In the course of his career, he fought for many employers, including the Visconti family, who ruled the city of Milan. When Muzio died in battle, his son Francesco (1401–1466) succeeded him as commander of his troops. While employed by Queen Giovanna of Naples, he left to fight for the Visconti against the Venetians. He was dismissed when the Visconti grew suspicious of his loyalties. But they soon needed him back, and as an inducement, he was promised the Visconti heir, Bianca Maria, as his wife. Mutual distrust still prevailed between Francesco and his future father-in-law, Filippo Maria, and it was years before the marriage took place. When Filippo died, Francesco wanted Filippo's dukedom. He ended up laying siege to Milan, which surrendered to him in 1450. He became a highly respected duke. He had numerous illegitimate children, as well as four children by Bianca Maria.

Francesco was succeeded by his son Galeazzo Maria, a cruel and dissolute ruler who was assassinated in 1476. Galeazzo Maria's heir, Gian Galeazzo, was only eight years old at the time, and it was Galeazzo Maria's brother Ludovico who finally controlled Milan after the resulting power struggle. Although he was supposedly Gian Galeazzo's guardian, Ludovico refused to give up power when Gian married Isabella of Naples in 1489, and a feud with Naples ensued. Ludovico began courting the French king, Charles VIII, who had claims to

Naples, in the hope that Charles would put an end to his troubles with Naples and with rival Venice. When Gian Galeazzo conveniently died soon after Charles' invasion in 1494, Ludovico become the uncontested ruler of Milan.

However, Ludovico soon found that he had made a serious mistake by encouraging the French invasion, because the Duke of Orleans, who would later become King Louis XII, had accompanied Charles to Italy and claimed Milan as his own because of his relationship to the Visconti family. Ludovico joined Pope Alexander VI and the other Italian powers to push Charles out of Italy. Louis XII returned to Milan and forced Ludovico to flee in 1499. Ludovico returned to power briefly in 1500, but was betrayed and taken prisoner by the French a few months later. He died in a French castle in 1508. After the departure of the French, the Sforza family ruled Milan with some interruptions until 1535.

Machiavelli mentions Ludovico with undisguised contempt, regarding him as one of the primary causes of Italy's misery. Ludovico was a plotter and intriguer, constantly making alliances and counter alliances that he imagined would propel him to greatness. He was ultimately undone by forces too powerful for him to manipulate. He was also a great patron of the arts. Leonardo da Vinci was in his employ at Milan for several years, and it was Ludovico who commissioned the painting of da Vinci's "Last Supper" for his favorite church.

Pope Julius II

Giuliano della Rovere (circa 1445–1513), the son of a poor family, was appointed cardinal over the church of San Pietro by his uncle, Pope Sixtus IV, in 1471. He became papal legate for his uncle, a position that took him on diplomatic missions to France and to the papal states. He was a bitter rival of Alexander VI, and by 1494, two years into the Borgia pope's reign, Giuliano left Rome, fearing for his life. He went to France, where he encouraged Charles VIII to press ahead with his plans for an Italian invasion, hoping to thereby depose Alexander. He accompanied Charles on his invasion and on his subsequent retreat. While in France, he judiciously welcomed Cesare Borgia's visit and even encouraged his conquest of the Romagna. He did not return to Rome until Alexander's death in 1503. He lacked the votes to get himself elected, but Alexander's pious and ascetic successor, Pius III, was in poor health and died after less than a month in office. Giuliano made a deal with Cesare Borgia, then desperate for allies, to get the votes of the Spanish cardinals, and became Pope Julius II on October 1, 1503.

Julius spent the majority of his papacy occupied by war, often appearing on the battlefield himself, wearing armor under his papal robes. Julius quickly disposed of Cesare, regardless of their arrangement, and set about putting the Romagna back under the control of the Papal States. The Venetians refused to give up several cities they had seized after Cesare's fall, so Julius formed the League of Cambrai, an alliance with Louis XII, Ferdinand of Spain, and Emperor Maximilian I, to defeat them. The Venetians surrendered, and Julius, chafing under the domination of Louis, formed an alliance with Venice and Switzerland to drive out the French. This alliance eventually included Ferdinand, Maximilian, and even Henry VII of England in what was called the "Holy League." The League's forces were defeated by the French at Ravenna in April 1512, but the demoralized French army subsequently withdrew, and the League proved victorious. Julius restored the Sforza to power in Milan and the Medici in Florence. He was turning his efforts against Spanish domination when he died unexpectedly in 1513. Machiavelli observes that the impetuous and energetic pope's unlikely successes probably could not have continued had he lived longer. Exhausted by Julius' military exploits and Alexander's debauchery, most Italians were pleased to see the milder Giovanni de Medici elected as Pope Leo X.

An indefatigable warrior and defender of the church's authority, Julius also adorned his church with grand works of art. He commissioned Michelangelo to paint the ceiling of the Sistine Chapel. A never-completed commission for Julius' monumental tomb produced some of Michelangelo's best sculpture. He hired Raphael, then in his 20s, to paint his new papal chambers, replacing pictures of the despised Borgias. Julius also began construction of what would become the present day church of St. Peter's in Rome.

CRITICAL
ESSAYS

Machiavelli the Devil

Few writers have inspired the kind of personal hatred that Machiavelli has throughout the centuries, and few works have been as vilified—or as popular—as *The Prince*. Machiavelli has been condemned as a defender of tyranny, a godless promoter of immorality, and a self-serving manipulator. Today, almost 500 years after *The Prince* was written, the dictionary still defines "Machiavellian" as "of, like, or characterized by the political principles and methods of expediency, craftiness, and duplicity set forth in Machiavelli's book, *The Prince*; crafty, deceitful, and so on." One popular, though untrue, story holds that "Old Nick," a slang term for the Devil, is derived from Machiavelli's first name, Niccolò.

Machiavelli's reputation as a diabolical figure began almost immediately after publication of *The Prince*. In 1559, not only *The Prince* but all of Machiavelli's works were placed on the Catholic church's "Index of Prohibited Books," presumably because of Machiavelli's perceived offenses against Christian ethics. Machiavelli has often been accused of being an atheist or even actively anti-Christian. His thinly veiled contempt for the papacy and the political ambitions of the Catholic church is evident in *The Prince*, and in the *Discourses*, he states that Christian piety robs its adherents of the energy necessary for the creation of a good society. Much of *The Prince* denies or even negates the moral basis of government that Christian thinkers insisted upon. The medieval Christian notion that good government is ordained by God for the promotion of virtue and the protection of the faithful against evil is distinctly absent from the world of *The Prince*. Perhaps more importantly, the quality that Machiavelli values most highly, *virtù*, is not a moral quality at all. Infamous criminals such as Agathocles or outrageously cruel rulers like Severus can still possess *virtù*. Debate continues as to whether Machiavelli can be called a Christian thinker or whether he adheres to some other standard of morality, such as those of the pagan Classical authors whose work he draws on. Some critics have proposed that Machiavelli simply substitutes an entirely new moral standard, one that is centered on the state, rather than on God or on pagan ethics.

While Machiavelli was officially banned in the Catholic world, he was also hated by the Protestants. In 1572, the Catholic leadership of France attempted to wipe out France's Protestant population, the Huguenots. In several weeks of massacres beginning on St.

Bartholomew's Day, an estimated 50,000 Huguenots were killed. The power behind the throne of France was Catherine de Medici, an Italian and a Catholic, and a member of the family for whom Machiavelli had written *The Prince*. Long-dead Machiavelli took blame for the incident, as it was supposed that Catherine had looked to his philosophies in planning the massacres. In Protestant England, Machiavelli became a stock character of evil on the theatrical stage. For example, in Christopher Marlowe's play *The Jew of Malta*, the character of "Machiavel" presents the prologue introducing the play's villainous title character, who gleefully follows Machiavellian precepts. To be so universally hated, however, Machiavelli also had to be widely read, as Marlowe's Machiavel points out: "Admir'd I am of those who hate me most. Though some speak openly against my books, Yet will they read me. . . ."

Of the many books specifically refuting *The Prince*, two deserve special mention. The first, written in 1576, was the *Discours sur les moyens de bien gouverner contre Nicolas Machiavel* by Innocent Gentillet. Gentillet, a Huguenot author protesting the St. Bartholomew's Day massacres, did more to establish Machiavelli's devilish reputation than did *The Prince* itself. The most famous response to *The Prince* came from Frederick the Great, King of Prussia. In 1740 he wrote, with the help of the French philosopher Voltaire, the *Anti-Machiavel*, a vigorous condemnation of Machiavelli's principles. Frederick, like many other royalists, feared the implication in *The Prince* that anyone who was strong enough to seize power was entitled to keep it, seeing it as an invitation to regicide. Ironically, Frederick would prove to be a true Machiavellian—treacherous, ruthless, and enthusiastic in his pursuit of power.

Modern scholars have applied a variety of interpretations to Machiavelli's work. Some view *The Prince* as an anti-Christian work, a celebration of Classical pagan philosophy, while others have attempted to portray Machiavelli as a Christian moralist, pointing out the political evils of the world around him. Some see *The Prince* as a book of despair, an anguished chronicle of fallen human nature, while others find in Machiavelli a clear-eyed realist and an accurate observer of the political sphere of life. Some have explained *The Prince*'s apparent immorality as amorality, a morally-neutral scientific analysis of the workings of politics, without approval or disapproval. More than one writer has proposed that *The Prince* is in fact a satire, a warning of what may happen if rulers are allowed to pursue power unchecked. In this view, Machiavelli is the passionate defender of republicanism, the champion of liberty, who describes the workings of tyranny so they can be resisted.

Others find in *The Prince* a blueprint for totalitarianism, carried to its logical and horrible conclusion in regimes like Nazi Germany or Stalinist Russia. Bertrand Russell called *The Prince* "a handbook for gangsters," and Leo Strauss called Machiavelli "a teacher of evil."

In more recent times, popular interest in Machiavelli's philosophy has focused more on money than on politics or morality. In an age in which democratic governments predominate, the last arena in which princely power can be pursued with abandon is that of business. Modern business executives seeking advice on effective leadership have resurrected Machiavelli, along with a host of other military and political strategists. One can find any number of contemporary advice books purporting to offer Machiavelli's insights, including *What Would Machiavelli Do?* (a devilish subversion of the popular catch-phrase "What would Jesus do?"), which may or may not be a satire.

Reason of State

The doctrine of "reason of state" is a slippery concept to define, having been used by many writers with different shades of meaning. In general, it refers to the idea that the well-being and stability of the state is paramount, and all of the government's actions should be directed to this end. This includes actions which would be considered illegal or immoral under ordinary circumstances. Machiavelli did not invent this doctrine, which can be found in the writings of many Classical authors, most notably, Tacitus. Machiavelli probably derived it from his study of Livy, Xenophon, and Aristotle. In fact, Machiavelli does not use the phrase "reason of state," which was first popularized by fellow Italian Giovanni Botero in his 1589 book, *Ragione de Stato*. Nonetheless, Botero's book draws heavily on Machiavelli's ideas, and Machiavelli is usually credited as the first modern writer to systematically describe the principles of reason of state.

Implicit throughout *The Prince* is the notion that almost any action of a ruler is justifiable if it contributes to the peace, prosperity, and stability of the state. Machiavelli endorses murder, deceit, violence, and cruelty, provided they are directed toward the greater good. He applauds Cesare Borgia's cruelty in subduing the Romagna because it ultimately brought peace and safety to the previously lawless region. In Machiavelli's defense, he does not endorse deceit or violence for its own sake. He assumes that there is a basic level of violence and injury that rulers cannot avoid. The key is to make the best use of this unavoidable cruelty. Actions that injure a few are better than actions that injure many. This principle can be seen in his discussion of colonies as a means of subduing a newly conquered territory. Colonies deprive a few people of their lands and homes, but they are preferable to occupation by an army, which injures and offends everyone in the territory. The greater good is clearly a consideration here. However, Machiavelli also makes clear his other primary consideration: The people who are injured by colonies are too few, too poor, and too scattered to pose any threat to the ruler who abuses them, while entire populations that hate and despise the new ruler are a definite threat to that ruler's continued power.

Botero accused Machiavelli of having a reason of state based on lack of conscience. Whether you accept Botero's judgment or not, he has pointed out the central problem with the concept: It is extremely difficult to separate reason of state from pure self-interest, and the questionable actions that promote the health of the state from those that promote the personal ambitions of the ruler. Because of this, reason of state has become associated with tyranny, and Machiavelli's brand in particular has been seen as a justification of absolutism and authoritarianism. Some critics have tried to defend Machiavelli by pointing out that *The Prince* is not a discourse on morality, but a purely technical, analytical study of political power. For this reason, Machiavelli is often described as the first true political scientist, someone who presented an impartial observation of politics as they truly are, rather than as theory dictated they should be. In doing so, he can be seen in the same light as Renaissance scientists like Galileo, who discarded traditional explanations of phenomena which were not consistent with their empirical observations of the workings of nature. In *The Prince*, the concept of the state has become autonomous and self-contained. Divorced from traditional Western concepts of Christian morality, it becomes an end unto itself, carrying along its own independent standard of behavior.

Reason of state fell out of fashion as a political philosophy by the end of the 17th century, but reappeared in the mid-19th century as *realpolitik*, a term often applied to the policies of German chancellor Otto von Bismarck. The dictionary defines realpolitik as "foreign policy determined by expediency rather than ethics or world opinion; power politics." The term is often translated as "practical politics," or politics that accomplish the goals of the state in the real world, rather than a world based on theory or idealism. One of the assumptions of realpolitik (or political Realism) is that all states act to maximize, or at least to preserve, their own power. Therefore, all international relations are based on a struggle for power. The opposing concept is Idealism, which assumes that different states have a basic harmony of interests. It is easy to see Machiavelli's influence on Realism, remembering his insistence that he would discuss things as they really are, as well as his strategic analysis of the best ways to acquire and keep power.

Virtù, Fortuna, and Free Will

The relationship between *virtù, fortuna*, and free will is one of the most interesting philosophical problems posed by *The Prince*. But Machiavelli probably did not intend to present a comprehensive philosophy that would explain human action and human failure; rather, he was simply making observations based on his own experience, and perhaps for this reason, his explanation is filled with contradictions.

The figure of the goddess *Fortuna*, luck or fortune, was derived from Classical Roman mythology, where she was often portrayed in a positive light. Though she was fickle and uncertain, she was also the bringer of good luck and abundance, and one of her symbols was an overflowing cornucopia. The Christian philosopher Boethius, however, focused on Fortuna's dark side in his *Consolation of Philosophy*, and although her Classical elements survived, subsequent images of her in medieval Europe focused on her ability to dash human hopes and ambitions. Her symbol was the turning wheel, which people rode to the top, only to be thrown to the bottom at the next turning. Fortuna embodied the tawdry and transitory glory of the world that the thoughtful Christian must seek to transcend by focusing on the unchangeable goods of virtue and faith, which had eternal glory in Heaven. The figure of Fortuna makes an appearance in Chapter 25 of *The Prince*, but the concept of fortune is present throughout. In general, Machiavelli uses *fortuna* to refer to all of those circumstances which human beings cannot control, and in particular, to the character of the times, which has direct bearing on a prince's success or failure. Whether fortune obeyed the will of God or was simply an impersonal natural force was a subject of debate throughout the Middle Ages and Renaissance. However, nowhere in *The Prince* is there an indication that one should try to transcend fortune; rather, one should meet it head on and bend it, if possible, to one's own will.

Virtù is the human energy or action that stands in opposition to fortune. While Machiavelli's use of the word does not exclude the idea of goodness or virtuous behavior, it does not necessarily include it, either.

Virtù is drive, talent, or ability directed toward the achievement of certain goals, and it is the most vital quality for a prince. Even criminals like Agathocles or extremely cruel rulers like Severus can possess *virtù*. Machiavelli sometimes seems to say that *virtù* could defeat *fortuna* if it was properly applied. If a prince could always adapt his *virtù* to the present circumstances, he would always be successful. Then again, Machiavelli implies that there is a connection between the two. In his statement that *virtù* is wasted if there is no opportunity, and opportunity is wasted if there is no *virtù*, Machiavelli implies that there is some kind of cooperation between the two forces—they cannot operate independently. It may not be possible to completely cancel out the effects of changing fortune, but by decisive action, it is possible to prepare for changes and to mitigate their bad effects.

Here lies the central contradiction of the philosophy. Machiavelli is quite specific in deciding that human beings do have free will; if they did not, energy and ability would be useless qualities. He admonishes the Medici by saying that God wants people to act, not to sit around waiting for things to happen. But Machiavelli also limits the power of free will to only half of human affairs; the other half, the realm of *fortuna*, cannot be controlled. The reasoning behind this remains obscure. Machiavelli says that people can only act according to their natures, which people are not flexible enough to alter. If, by nature, a prince is impetuous, and the times are ripe for impetuous action, the prince will be successful; but when the times change, a prince cannot change his natures with them, and this brings about his failure. Because a prince can neither choose his nature nor change it, free will seems illusory indeed, and *virtù*, for all its admirability, begins to look like a cruel trick played by God, or Fortuna, or some other uncontrollable force, on humankind. Although Machiavelli seeks to deny fatalism, he also seems to argue himself into it. Many critics have found in Chapter 25 of *The Prince* the lowest depths of Machiavelli's cynicism, because the logical conclusion of his argument is that nothing the prince does particularly matters, because he is a mere political time server.

If this is really his final conclusion, however, Machiavelli scarcely seems aware of it, and it does nothing to dampen the enthusiasm of his plea to the Medici to liberate Italy. It is difficult to accept that Machiavelli would spend so much effort honing his sharp advice to the prince if there is no real point in following it. This apparent contradiction has kept readers debating over the real meaning of Machiavelli's philosophy for centuries.

CliffsNotes Review

Use this CliffsNotes Review to test your understanding of the original text and reinforce what you've learned in this book. After you work through the review and essay questions and the fun and useful practice projects, you're well on your way to understanding a comprehensive and meaningful interpretation of *The Prince*.

Q&A

1. What are the types of principalities that Machiavelli discusses?

2. Does Machiavelli discuss republics in *The Prince*?

3. Which conqueror in Machievelli's time does he offer as a model of princely behavior?

4. What are the different types of troops Machiavelli mentions? Which kind are most useful?

5. What animals should the prince imitate?

6. What are the different methods by which a new principality can be acquired?

7. Which of the following qualities should the prince possess: generosity, stinginess, cruelty, mercy, trustworthiness, deceit.

8. It is better to be _____ than to be loved.

9. What sort of advisors should a prince avoid?

10. When should a prince build fortresses?

Answers: (1) Hereditary, mixed, new, and ecclesiastical. (2) No. He discusses only principalities. (3) Cesare Borgia. (4) Mercenaries, auxiliaries, mixed troops, and native troops. Native troops are the most useful. (5) The fox, for cunning, and the lion, for strength. (6) By one's own power, by the power of others, by criminal acts, or by the will of the people. (7) The prince should prefer stinginess over generosity, cruelty over mercy, and deceit over trustworthiness. (8) Feared. (9) Flatterers. (10) When he fears his own people more than he fears foreign invaders.

Essay Questions

1. Describe the qualities of Machiavelli's ideal prince. What characteristics should a prince possess, and how should a prince behave?

2. Discuss the concept of *fortuna*. How does Machiavelli use this term? What can be done to resist *fortuna*?

3. Examine the instances in which Machiavelli discuss "the people." What is his attitude toward the people and their interests? How does he portray them? How does he portray their opposites, the nobles?

4. Describe Machiavelli's concept of free will. How is *virtù* involved in this concept? According to Machiavelli, to what extent can free will be effectively exercised?

5. Why is the prince's public image important to Machiavelli? What should a prince do to maintain a good reputation? How should the prince present himself to the people he rules?

Practice Projects

1. Imagine that you work for a company that is managed entirely on the principles outlined in *The Prince*. What would this company be like? Describe it from the point of view of an entry-level employee. How would this person be treated, and what could they expect from the company? Then describe it from the point of view of an executive. How would this executive view the employees, and what would this executive's relations with others be like? Consider the company's competitors. If they were also Machiavellian companies, what would interactions between the companies be like? How would a non-Machiavellian company fare against a Machiavellian one?

2. Outline and discuss Machiavelli's assumptions about violence and the use of force in The Prince. What does he see as the role of force in a society? How should force be used or controlled? Then compare this view with that of a noted non-violent leader (the best known examples are Martin Luther King, Jr., or Mahatma Gandhi, but you may choose any leader who promoted a philosophy of non-violence or non-resistance). To do so, you will need to outline that leader's non-violent philosophy. On what points do these two different philosophies disagree? Are there any points on which they agree? Finally, which philosophy do you find more effective for governing a society? Can violence be completely eliminated from government? If not, how can it best be managed?

CliffsNotes Resource Center

The learning doesn't need to stop here. CliffsNotes Resource Center shows you the best of the best links to the best information in print and online about the author and/or related works. And don't think that this is all we've prepared for you; we've put all kinds of pertinent information at www.cliffsnotes.com. Look for all the terrific resources at your favorite bookstore or local library and on the Internet. When you're online, make your first stop www.cliffsnotes.com where you'll find more incredibly useful information about Machiavelli and *The Prince*.

Books

This CliffsNotes book, published by IDG Books Worldwide, Inc., provides a meaningful interpretation of *The Prince*. If you are looking for information about the author and/or related works, check out these other publications:

DE GRAZIA, SEBASTIAN. *Machiavelli in Hell*. Princeton, NJ: Princeton University Press, 1989. A scholarly book written in an almost novelistic style. Not strictly a biography, it is an exploration of Machiavelli's thought, portraying him as a Christian moralist.

NAJEMY, JOHN M., et al. "Machiavelli, Niccolò." *Encyclopedia of the Renaissance*. Ed. Paul F. Grandler. 6 vols. New York: Scribner's, 1999. A handy introduction to Machiavelli's life, works, and influence, with a useful bibliography.

PAREL, ANTHONY, ed. *The Political Calculus*. Toronto: University of Toronto Press, 1972. A collection of essays on basic Machiavellian themes. The essays on necessity, *virtù*, and *fortuna* are especially helpful.

PITKIN, HANNA FENICHEL. *Fortune is a Woman: Gender and Politics in the Thought of Machiavelli*. Berkeley, CA: University of California at Berkeley Press, 1984. A study of the role of women and the use of feminine imagery in Machiavelli's writings.

RIDOLFI, ROBERTO. *The Life of Niccolò Machiavelli*. Trans. Cecil Grayson. Chicago: University of Chicago Press, 1963. Still the standard biography of Machiavelli in English. Very readable and extensively footnoted.

SKINNER, QUENTIN. *Machiavelli*. Rev. ed. Oxford: Oxford University Press, 1985. A good general introduction to the body of Machiavelli's thought.

STRAUSS, LEO. *Thoughts on Machiavelli*. Glencoe, IL: Free Press, 1958. The most eloquent of the modern critics who consider Machiavelli immoral.

It's easy to find books published by IDG Books Worldwide, Inc. and other publishers. You'll find them in your favorite bookstores (on the Internet and at a store near you). IDG Books also has three Web sites that you can use to read about all the books we publish:

- www.cliffsnotes.com
- www.dummies.com
- www.idgbooks.com

Magazines and Journals

Berlin, Isaiah. "The question of Machiavelli." *New York Review of Books*. November 4, 1971: pp. 20–32. Expanded and reprinted as "The Originality of Machiavelli" in *Against the Current: Essays in the History of Ideas*. Ed. Henry Hardy. New York: Viking, 1980. pp. 25–79. An excellent overview of the varied interpretations applied to Machiavelli, with the author's own thoughtful analysis.

Price, Russell. "The senses of *virtù* in Machiavelli." *European Studies Review* (1973). pp. 315–45. An examination of one of Machiavelli's most difficult concepts.

Internet

For someone who has inspired so much interest and controversy, Machiavelli is unfortunately under-represented on the Internet. Students looking for critical evaluations of Machiavelli's works are probably better served by consulting print sources. However, the constantly changing state of the Internet means that more useful resources may appear in the future.

Electronic versions of some of Machiavelli's works, particularly *The Prince*, can be found on the Internet. For a selection, consult *Project Gutenberg*, available at `http://sailor.gutenberg.org` or `http://www.gutenberg.net`. A more comprehensive listing of electronic texts is available at the *On-Line Books Page*, `http://digital.library.upenn.edu/books/`.

A brief listing of Web pages related to Machiavelli is available at About.com's *Who's Who in Medieval History?* site, found at `http://historymedren.about.com/homework/historymedren/library/who/blwmachia.htm`.

One of the best informed articles about Machiavelli on the Web is provided by the online version of *The Catholic Encyclopedia*, found at `www.newadvent.org/cathen/09501a.htm`.

Next time you're on the Internet, don't forget to drop by `www.cliffsnotes.com`. We've created an online Resource Center that you can use today, tomorrow, and beyond.

Send Us Your Favorite Tips

In your quest for knowledge, have you ever experienced that sublime moment when you figure out a trick that saves time or trouble? Perhaps you realized you were taking ten steps to accomplish something that could have taken two. Or you found a little-known workaround that achieved great results. If you've discovered a useful tip that helped you read and understand Niccolò Machiavelli and *The Prince* more effectively and you'd like to share it, the CliffsNotes staff would love to hear from you. Go to our Web site at `www.cliffsnotes.com` and click the Talk to Us button. If we select your tip, we may publish it as part of CliffsNotes Daily, our exciting, free e-mail newsletter. To find out more or to subscribe to a newsletter, go to `www.cliffsnotes.com` on the Web.

NOTES

NOTES

NOTES

NOTES

NOTES

NOTES

NOTES

@ cliffsnotes.com

CliffsNotes™
@ cliffsnotes.com

Check Out the All-New CliffsNotes Guides

TECHNOLOGY TOPICS

Balancing Your Checkbook with Quicken
Buying and Selling on eBay
Buying Your First PC
Creating a Winning PowerPoint 2000 Presentation
Creating Web Pages with HTML
Creating Your First Web Page
Exploring the World with Yahoo!
Getting on the Internet
Going Online with AOL
Making Windows 98 Work for You

Setting Up a Windows 98 Home Network
Shopping Online Safely
Upgrading and Repairing Your PC
Using Your First iMac
Using Your First PC
Writing Your First Computer Program

PERSONAL FINANCE TOPICS

Budgeting & Saving Your Money
Getting a Loan
Getting Out of Debt
Investing for the First Time
Investing in 401(k) Plans
Investing in IRAs
Investing in Mutual Funds
Investing in the Stock Market
Managing Your Money
Planning Your Retirement
Understanding Health Insurance
Understanding Life Insurance

CAREER TOPICS

Delivering a Winning Job Interview
Finding a Job on the Web
Getting a Job
Writing a Great Resume